Praise for *The Grandma Boom Chronicles*

I hope all can learn from this  *of life has its ups, downs, and* *It made me feel young at hear*

> ~ Doris Da
> Hollywoc ﹍﹍
> and animal welfare activist

Janai Mestrovich's eccentric, charming, and cross-generational stories are an entertaining and inspiring read. There's enlightened wisdom in here for anyone—both old and young.

> ~ Danny Lockwood
> Music video producer for musicians
> and celebrities including Katy Perry,
> Jennifer Lopez, and Bruce Springsteen

Janai Mestrovich is a blessing to this planet. Her work with children, especially very young children, is thoroughly useful, up to date with early childhood research, and yet uniquely hers. Her written work is carefully tuned to the complex learning patterns of children and avoids the dry lecture tone of many school curricula.

I had the privilege of helping Janai get started with guided imagery work many years ago and I believe she is exceptionally gifted intuitively. She has taken off and has never turned back. With remarkable lightness, creativity, and immense courage, in the 35 years I have known Janai, I have never seen her waiver from her altruistic path.

> ~ Dr. Stuart Twemlow
> Internationally recognized speaker, and
> 2012 recipient of the *Sigourney Award for
> Distingushed Contributions to the
> Field of Psychoanalysis*

Janai Mestrovich brings her upbeat energy, passion, and creativity to everything she does in her work and in her life. Rich in imagination, intuition, and flair, she embodies holistic education and inspires and delights both children and adults. Her stories in The Grandma Boom Chronicles *are infused with her resilient, positive spirit and her passion for promoting transformation and hope.*

> ~ RONI ADAMS, PH.D.
>   School of Education
>   Southern Oregon University

the GRANDMA BOOM chronicles

More Alive at 65!

Janai Mestrovich
aka Grandma Boom

Janai Mestrovich
Grandma Boom Publications
Ashland, Oregon 97520
www.grandmaboom.com

Cover and interior design: Chris Molé Design

Developmental and managing editor: Patricia Florin

Proofreading: Larissa Kyzer

Back cover photograph: Pam Danielle

ISBN: 978-0692274385

Manufactured in the United States of America
10 9 8 7 6 5 4 3 2 1

DEDICATION

This book is lovingly dedicated to children and the inner children of all ages. May we joyfully attain our greatest potential while remaining creatively playful and full of wonder. May an attitude of gratitude keep our spirits uplifted with abundant blessings.

FOREWORD

I have known Janai Mestrovich for six decades. As her sister, I have witnessed her go through loss, rejection, struggle, and suffering. I have experienced her emerge from the depths of these trials with even more compassion, sensitivity, joy, creativity, humor, and passion for truly living life with enthusiasm, pizzazz, vitality, and commitment. She is an incredibly dedicated individual and devotes herself to creating and promoting positive change. These virtues and attributes sparkle and shine in her work with adults and children alike. Janai is a mover, a shaker, and is steadfast and unhesitating in her focus and devotion for personal and global transformation. She is one who can truly bloom wherever she is planted.

Karen Mestrovich Seay
Co-Owner and Office Manager,
Regulator Time Company

"What comes from the Heart
goes to the Heart."

~ COLERIDGE

SPECIAL NOTE FROM THE AUTHOR

Empowering children and the inner child of all ages is my passion. I encourage others to expand their human potential by first transforming the way they experience past events that have depleted their strength to move forward in the evolution of who they can become. This includes learning to accept and nurture our natural, intuitive nature and getting in touch with our inner child, which is an essential part of living our truth and feeling the wonder of life.

My own story tells the journey of a repressed child who grew up in the 1950s and learned to change her destiny. The 1960s open my sheltered eyes and expanded possibilities both in the world around me and in the world inside me. I began to connect with the spirit of who I am. I sought to know how to fit the pieces of my life-puzzle together in a way that made sense and gave me purpose and meaning. Becoming a mom and grandmom were dreams-come-true and added tremendous depth and texture to my journey. Aging brings wonderful challenges that I choose to harness with gratitude and a positive attitude, youthening my spirit.

Finding the keys to happiness was a struggle, but it has brought great rewards. My spirituality has been transformed several times over as I leapt from a Croatian

Catholic upbringing to exploring philosophies and spiritual practices from all over the world. I studied with Tibetan lamas, Native American medicine women, Asian and Indian gurus, and lay people who attained wisdom through their own searches. I continue to gather healing tools for self-help and spiritual growth that can benefit me and others, and my home is filled with symbols from many uplifting practices that keep me motivated to integrate what I learn into my daily reality.

I intersperse the telling of my story with present-day pieces to show how the past can be used consciously to guide our actions in the present. For me, the connections between past and present are particularly clear now that I am a grandmother.

I hope you see in this self-help memoir ways to help yourself reframe painful experiences, connect with your inner child, and heal. I wish you a wonderful experience reading my offerings in this book. May you be happy in your heart and spirit.

Grandma Boom

Out of respect for the privacy for certain individuals, fictitious names are used.

TABLE OF CONTENTS

CHAPTER 1

Connections to Grandparenting

The puppy dogs that weren't

Seeing my Croatian grandmother dressed only in a half-slip when I was three years old was purely accidental, as my family was extremely private. I remember calling and looking for Mama, as everyone, including Papa (my grandfather), called my grandmother. She wasn't in the kitchen or the living room. Her bedroom door was closed. Even though I was taught to knock, finding Mama was more important, and I opened the door.

I was so excited when I saw her. "MAMA! Where did you get those puppy dogs?" Mama's puppy dogs started jiggling all over her chest from her full-bodied laughter. But she did not answer me. Giggling, she scooted me out of the room and shut the door. I didn't understand. Where in the world did she get those puppies? Why hadn't she let me play with them? They looked like what we called "wiener dogs" back then. And hers had big noses!

Many years later I learned that Mama did not wear underwear. When I had walked in and saw her long breasts, I had thought they were puppy dogs, and she was unable to explain to me in her broken English what I was seeing. Moreover, even if she could have spoken clearly, she would not have explained. Hers was the "ignore and it will go away" approach.

Mama always wore a dress. It was the Croatian woman's way. For a long time after the puppy dog incident, I would look at her chest and wonder why she would not share her puppies with me. Whenever I asked her about it, she giggled, which made her puppy dogs jiggle. Eventually, I gave up asking about them. I imagine she was quite relieved.

Some precious moments between grandchildren and grandparents cannot be fully appreciated in real time. Reflecting and savoring those special moments in the memory brings about a full-bodied appreciation in the heart and soul. An all-pervasive warmth reels in my recollections of Mama. I knew that she loved me and would always love me no matter what I did or said. It was the kind of love that provides the comfort of a cozy blanket on a cold winter day. That is how it felt to be with Mama. Always.

Remembrances of being three and having an unusual experience with my own grandmother brought to mind an unforgettable incident with my grandson shortly before he turned three. Now I would be the grandparent who was embarrassed.

Jackson's compassion and an unexpected outcome

One day when I was to care for my grandson, Jackson, I purchased a doll with a zipper, button, etc. to help him learn how to dress himself. I planned to combine that with a lesson on the theme of compassion. What I had in mind was preparing him for the imminent arrival of his baby sister.

So, pretending I dropped the doll, I picked it up and hugged it, saying, "Oh, I have so much compassion for the baby doll. She fell and got hurt." Jackson clumsily tried to say "compassion" and asked me what that meant. I hugged the dolly again and told him I knew what it felt like to get hurt, so I wanted to be kind to her and help her. I dropped the dolly again and Jackson took the initiative and repeated what I had done. I complimented him on his compassion for the baby-doll and said it was good she felt his compassion and knew he understood how she felt.

After that, we played with his train set. To be at his eye level, I knelt on the hard tile floor. After an hour, tired of kneeling, I told him I needed to change position, and I got up, one foot stepping to the side to leverage lifting the other knee off the floor. As my knee pushed me upward, relieving the pressure on my torso, an accidental toot squeaked out. From across the train table, Jackson's eyes popped open. "Grandma Boom, we need to CHANGE you!"

I came unglued. What followed was a conversation a grandma does not ever want to have with her grandchild. "Oh, no, Jackson, Grandma did not poop in her pants. It was just a toot! You know, a fart toot!" He looked at me with discerning eyes. I continued. "I really didn't poop in my pants and I don't need to be changed, Jackson. But thank you for having compassion and wanting to help. That is so nice of you."

A flashback of the incident with Mama nudged me gently, and I appreciated making the choice to communicate with Jackson, even though it *was* embarrassing. And then I changed the subject.

Jackson may not remember this incident as he grows older, but he will have experiences that strike his fancy and won't be forgotten. Certain scenes from my past, even from toddlerhood, remain with me and pop up in association with something said, or with a picture, or with an aroma, and that time of my life blends with the present moment in conspicuous ways.

Shadow fear

I have learned that life consists of two primary emotional experiences: love and fear. All other emotions are offshoots of these. Doses of both love and fear penetrated my childhood. Courage was born from hearing fear's signal, and courage moved me ahead in spite of fear because my love of someone or something was greater. Sometimes, fear appeared as the saving grace from a pain so deep that nothing could heal it except the courage to change. Mom always said, "When the pain we bear becomes greater than the pain of change, we change."

One of my strongest memories when I was a toddler was in Mama and Papa's front yard on Strawberry Hill, the

Croatian settlement in Kansas City, Kansas, where my Dad grew up. The memory is twofold.

"AHHHHHHHHHH!!!!" When remembering this experience, I hear myself screaming and feel the extreme fear that shot through my body that day. I was trying to get away from the dark monster that was chasing me. While my little body-self ran and screamed near the house, I also watched from outside of my body as some part of me hovered near the edge of the yard. It was my first out-of-body experience, something I didn't comprehend at the time. (Even if I had told them about it, my parents would have raised their eyebrows, rolled their eyes, and brushed it under the rug.)

Anyway, I could not escape the dark monster and I was horrified. And why was everyone laughing at me? Dad finally came over and showed me that I was afraid of my own shadow. I'm sure I didn't understand his words at the time. With his own hand he showed me how shadows move as our bodies move. The part of me that hovered at the edge of the yard and above the scene watched this like it was a movie, until Dad touched my hand, and suddenly, the movie-watching stopped; I was back *in* the movie, feeling his hand guide mine to make shadows with his, and I understood.

Perhaps that shadow fear created the repeating dream that haunted my childhood. I would awaken with my heart beating fast as monsters chased me up a mountain. No matter what I tried, I could not escape the sound of their footfalls, their grunting, and the feeling of their hot breath on my back. I never was able to see them, but I knew they were there, trying hard to get me. Running uphill to escape them, I would become breathless. Then I would wake up, with my heart beating like mad. This vivid, frequent, precisely repeating dream was a part of my childhood landscape. I didn't know how to get rid of it or how to get help.

As an adult, a memory surfaced of something that happened when I was ten, and I believe it was the coming-to-life of my unresolved recurring dream of being chased by monsters. I was roller skating and stopped to rest on the bumper of a car. With growing alarm, I looked around and realized I had sat on a wasp nest. I charged home, over a block away. They chased me. Being on roller skates, I was limited in movement and could not elude them, just as I could not elude the monsters in my dream. My fear was uncontrollable, making me more vulnerable. Eleven stings were found on my body. There is a saying that fear attracts energy to manifest itself. I have seen evidence of that more than once.

My grandson had fearful monster nightmares. I began doing artwork with him and talking about the bad dreams as I have with many children. As we began processing the bad dreams, I deeply understood his fear and what it was like to be trapped in a dream without recourse. In my creative therapeutic work over the decades, I helped many children with this same issue.

We did artwork so he could see his feelings inside the dream and release them. We acted out the dreams, switching roles and feeling the power of making the monster go away. It took time.

I told Jackson he could call on me in his nightmare and I would come help him. The next night the bad dream recurred. He reported I was at the ocean shore with him. A big sea dragon monster came out of the water. He told me to get behind him and he would save me. He pulled out his sea dragon monster sword and cut the monster into pieces, then threw them back into the sea. When Jackson finished telling me about it, I praised his courage—and for saving me in the dream. He was beyond proud of the fact that he got rid of the monster and was strong enough to save his Grandma Boom.

Jackson had needed to feel purpose, in this case to protect me, in order to feel his own strength and courage. His bad dreams subsided. It was a tremendous accomplishment on his part. I was able to help my grandson with something I wish could have been there for me in my childhood. What a great thing it is to be on that side of a gift, that even though I hadn't received what I craved, at least I could give it!

"It's never too late to
have a happy childhood."

~ TOM ROBBINS, author
Still Life with Woodpecker

CHAPTER 2

Background DNA:
Fear, Courage, and Love

My recurring nightmare demonstrates how much fear I felt growing up. I was afraid of so many things: death, getting in trouble, and going to hell and being too hot, being near horned, ugly creatures, and melting like the wicked witch in *Wizard of Oz*. I was afraid of the humiliation and pain of being spanked and beaten. I was scared to death that Mom was going to hell because she wasn't a Catholic and that I'd never see her in heaven. Afraid I would do something wrong and be told I was stupid (a common occurrence). Afraid others wouldn't like me, afraid to speak up, afraid I wouldn't count as being good enough to go to heaven, afraid I wasn't perfect enough to be lovable. At that time, I saw fear in everyone, each person afraid for different reasons. And I saw courage. Love was present, radiating its light into the mix of emotions that darkened our souls.

Of all the fears that haunted me, one has nipped at my heels more painfully than any other. Ever since I was very young, I wanted to be the best little girl I could be and I was afraid of not accomplishing what I was supposed to with my life. A nagging sensation drove me to continually seek out what I was supposed to do. Who was I? Why was I born? Even though I sensed I was born to help, exactly HOW was I supposed to help? Was my potential limited, a sealed deal, or was it unlimited, with freedom in its core? Perplexed about my life's purpose, I watched family members for clues.

I knew my grandparents had accomplished a great feat. They had escaped from a dictatorship to a free country. They longed to give a good life to their children and grandchildren. In turn, my dad, fearing freedom would again be taken from his loved ones, helped protect them by going as a soldier to fight Hitler's regime.

Papa (Marko) Mestrovich, my grandfather, had mustered up the determination and courage to leave his family, his country, and his friends in his homeland of Croatia. He also left Mama (Katarina), although they were betrothed. It took him eleven years to work, save money, build a home. He then sent money for Mama to join him in marriage on Strawberry Hill in Kansas City. Courage and love brought them the hope of a new home and a new life. He overcame the fear, which had driven him to go beyond what he had known, and he would never return to his homeland.

Courage is a decision we make. I saw that fear could freeze-frame an issue and hold it fast, blocking movement and change. But my relatives had used fear as a stimulus for courage. Papa's courage filtered down through his descendants. This tendency was imparted to me. I wondered if it was also in my DNA, like my blue eyes and high forehead. I wanted to know how it felt to have the courage to answer my calling, like Papa did.

Mama was courageous, too. When I was a girl, she told me about having one trunk of belongings when she came on the boat across the great sea to reach Papa on Strawberry Hill. She was on the lower deck, which was uncovered. The boat was crowded. People who were sick on the upper deck would vomit over the side, and sometimes it would land on the passengers on the lower deck. It happened to her. For bathroom needs, buckets were provided. It was not an easy journey. She was afraid. And yet she had the courage to go, alone, with no help. She was motivated by her love for Papa and by her fear of living in a dictatorship.

Mama's boat journey was imprinted on me. I thought of her making that journey alone. Often, I felt alone, like a vat waiting for something to pour into me and give me fullness. I also felt I needed someone to save me—God, Jesus, angels, humans, I didn't know. It wasn't until later in life that I realized I had to save myself—only then could I begin to realize my potential. Meanwhile, I had to find my way, step by step, through the mire of well-intentioned but dysfunctional family and life dynamics.

Mama and Papa had a set arrangement: What Papa said became the rule of the house and Mama had no power. None. Financially and verbally she was submissive. Sometimes she was able to get what she wanted by sneaky methods, a skill she mastered. Nothing was ill-intentioned. It was just survival.

During my early years, Mama and Papa lived on Strawberry Hill, a Croatian settlement in Kansas City, Kansas. Their oldest son, Uncle Mark, and their middle child, a daughter, Aunt Kay, lived with them. Dad was their youngest. On Strawberry Hill, Mama and Papa introduced me to friendship with animals. They had two Dalmatians, Junior and Freckles. Those furry friends taught me about connecting with the heart. Even though we "spoke different languages," I felt protected and loved. They accepted me as I was. They were family.

When I was in grade school, Mama, Papa, Uncle Mark, and Aunt Kay moved to Miros Circle, where we lived, in order to be near our family. The government had forced them to move. The Strawberry Hill houses were destroyed in order to improve road conditions between the Kansas and Missouri border. Although it was difficult for them to leave their home, this event created the opportunity for them to be in frequent contact with Dad and his budding family.

Seeds of gratitude

When I was young, Mama helped me to understand the importance of gratitude. It was to become a saving, enlightening grace for my life journey. It creates the foundation for a positive attitude and is vital as I develop and realize my potential.

"Honey," Mama would tell me, "on Christmas Day I get one orange or apple in old country. That was special. We have not much money. I was happy to have orange or apple once a year on Christmas." Mama often shared bits and pieces of her life in the old country. One of Mama's expressions of gratitude was to scrape all the scraps on our plates onto hers at the end of a meal. Even if she was full, she would eat every morsel. She refused to waste anything. I remember feeling awed as I watched, and secretly hoped she would not burst.

Mama also gave me a gift when she taught me to bake Croatian egg bread, apple strudel, povetica (walnut bread), homemade noodles, and other tasty dishes. In the midst of helping her bake and getting to eat lots of dough, Mama taught me how to bless the food. In a moment of silence, she would make the sign of the cross. A peaceful feeling would wash over me during her blessing. Then she would say, "If you are fortunate enough to have the ingredients to bake, always share, because it keeps you humble and grateful." I agreed to do that. And I do. It is an invaluable gift that Mama planted in my heart. When I bake, she is with me.

Mom meets Dad

Mom (Carolyn Harrison) met Dad (John Jan Mestrovich) when he was stationed in the Army during World War II near Wildwood, Florida, her hometown. Mom was married at the time to RG. Dad was RG's commanding officer. My parents met when RG was hospitalized and Mom went to see RG in his hospital room. It was Dad's responsibility to tell her that her husband was ill with syphilis. RG improved and returned to the house where my mom and RG lived.

Soon afterward, Mom's dad was killed at the railroad where he worked, run over by a train. When Mom was notified about his death, she left her own work to tell RG. That's when she found him in bed with another woman. She would remember it as one of the horrible moments in her life. Beside herself, she moved back to live with her mother, Ida Harrison (whom I would later call Big Mama).

After the funeral, Mom decided to divorce RG. During the process, there was pressure from her community for her to stay married to him. One evening, in front of Big Mama's house, the Ku Klux Klan showed up, threatening her if she divorced. It was hellishly frightening for Mom and Big Mama as they watched the white-garbed men holding their fiery torches and listened to them threaten their lives. The KKK wanted to make sure Mom didn't go through with the divorce.

RG's friends and relatives were heavily invested in the KKK. Mom knew that. Although frightened to death, Mom would not give in. She continued with the divorce process. Fortunately, the KKK did not make another nocturnal visit. Mom's courage to follow through with the divorce conquered her fear of the KKK. I respect her for not succumbing to their threats, even though she knew she could have been in harm's way. Not allowing them to control her life, she moved forward with strength and a new direction.

As Mom divorced RG, Dad was sent overseas. They had flirted and were attracted to each other. Mom said that she was excited when she received the first letter from Dad. Their correspondence built fondness. When Dad returned from the WWII, he was stationed in Los Alamos, New Mexico. He sent a letter to Mom, asking her to join him.

She quit her job and left immediately.

John Jan Mestrovich and Carolyn Harrison were married on June 21, 1947 in Santa Fe, New Mexico. They enjoyed a wedding dinner at the La Fonda Hotel. Life was good and exciting. They had a horse named Star, and a Native American maid, Nettie, with whom Mom grew close. Mom and Dad were the first white people to be invited to an all-night Native American ceremony. On that night, Nettie's father, the Chief, let Mom and Dad see the walking cane that President Lincoln had given to his father.

Mom and Dad never shared details about the ceremony except to say it was special to be invited. They felt honored. My sense is that a seed was planted in both of them about spirituality versus religion. Mom, of English, Irish, French, and Native American descent, was raised strictly as a Southern Baptist. Dad's background was full-blooded Croatian Roman Catholic. Native Americans were considered savages by many in the white community, so Mom hid the fact from all of us that she was part Native American until we were adults. At the time, it was not in vogue to be anything but white. Yet that all-night ceremony had given them a feeling for what moved others into a sacred space. Whenever they spoke of it, their voices had a reverent tone.

Mom had a miscarriage soon after she and Dad married. A short time later, I was conceived at Los Alamos, where they lived. It tickles me to think I came in with the atomic energy. When unexplainable things have happened in my life, I credit Los Alamos. Ha-ha!

After I was conceived, Mom and Dad moved to Ames, Iowa. Dad wanted to complete the engineering degree he had begun before the war. He was tested at Iowa State, and the professors considered his gifts to be prodigious. He earned, with honors, a degree in Civil Engineering.

During the pregnancy and while Dad went to school, Mom typed for twenty-five cents an hour. Money was tight. Mom said she craved strawberries during the entire pregnancy, but they could not afford to buy even one. I was born with a strawberry imprint on my right cheek, and Mom said it was because she craved them. My body size was smaller than the rest of my siblings to come. My health was poor and my hair was thinner than that of my brothers and sisters.

Mom had fallen down some stairs while she was pregnant with me. That triggered the onset of us laboring together for my birth. On several occasions throughout my life I asked Mom to please tell me about my birth. She would never tell me details. Her response was always, "You don't want to know. It was too horrible." My overriding sense is that I died while being born. I have always had a hang-up about being dunked in a pool or being grabbed by my neck. I've never liked going under water. I wonder if I felt like I was drowning in amniotic fluid and the umbilical cord was wrapped around my neck.

Six weeks after I was born, Mom took me and left Dad, running back to Wildwood, Florida, where Big Mama still lived in a white frame house. It had a small front porch with a wooden rocker. The sandy yard had biting red ants. Upon arriving at Big Mama's house, Mom's milk dried up in the middle of the night, making me a fussy baby. She didn't understand at the time why it had happened. (In later years, she learned that stress can have an impact on the body.)

Dad refused to accept that Mom left, and on a break between semesters, he drove from Ames to Wildwood and convinced her to return with him. But it wasn't long before she ran away again. Again he convinced her to return, only this time to Kansas City, Kansas, with promises of a happy life.

With Mom and Dad's relationship as the driving force in our family life, strife, anger, fear, and a lack of communication skills wove themselves into our family. This tumultuous ground had tremendous impact on all four of us kids. While Mom and Dad had a strong attraction to each other, they also triggered each other's dark sides. We lived in a double bind, a situation of "damned if you do and damned if you don't."

St. John the Baptist Parish

St. John the Baptist Parish, kindergarten, grade school, and nunnery were the glue that held the Croatian settlement together. All the nuns and priests spoke Croatian and English. Dad had had the same kindergarten teacher, Sister Proxeda, that I did. He actually had to learn English when he went to school. Experiences such as ice cream socials and events at the church, the bowling alley, and the playground allowed both young and old to participate. Church services were the most treasured, but the ice cream socials were the most fun. Once my dad held me, dancing all around the church hall to a polka played by a man with an accordion. I was up high with Dad, being swung around while we both laughed. To a little girl, not even ice cream could measure up in joy.

St. John the Baptist Parish also sponsored an orphanage that was part of the convent where the nuns lived. I volunteered when I was in grade school to go help with the orphans. I felt so sorry for them. I picked up on a feeling in that dimly lit, smelly orphanage, a feeling of emptiness. I'm not so sure that the nuns were warm and comforting caretakers. I wanted to give the children something that felt good—a hug or a smile. The dishes, cups, and silverware on the shelves were often dirty and sticky. The orphans were often sick. It was a situation in which I could help, and that always helped me feel better about myself.

It fascinated me how the nuns stood straighter and walked stiffer than the priests. The nuns also looked flat-chested and I wondered: Did being flat-chested mean one had to become a nun? I hoped I would fill out. In my young mind, I noticed that the nuns moved in angular ways, and I figured that, hidden under their habits, were suspenders or chains that connected their underwear.

For many years, the nuns, wearing rigidity as an everyday robe, were a regular influence in my life. They did not look happy. Some angered easily. I would have given anything to see them on the playground with their students in a game of Red Rover, sock ball, or jump rope.

The fourth-grade teacher, Sister Amancha, acted as if she had persistent PMS. Most days, violence transpired in her classroom. Children's knuckles were rendered raw from Sister Amancha's ruler. Sometimes her miserable reality exploded like an angry geyser, and she threw books, heavy bells, erasers, chalk—anything she could easily grab. When I saw the pitch of her arm raise and an object in her hand, I ducked. Many times she hit her target. Sometimes she missed the intended student, someone who was whispering or scribbling, and hit an innocent bystander. One of my friends was hit. Her parents moved her to a different school the next day. Nuns were instruments of God, so there were no consequences for their violent behaviors, at least not ones that were obvious to us. Obedience and respecting one's elders were the drums we marched to.

Even though God and Church were highly respected in the Croatian settlement, humans were human, and to survive, they did what they to do. At an early age, Dad was trained by Papa to help bring in money for the family in ways that would have been considered less-than-honorable by many members of the holy cloth.

Way of life on Strawberry Hill

"I drove Papa's car across the Kansas State line into Missouri by myself when I was seven years old." Dad was proud of that accomplishment. On Strawberry Hill during Prohibition, Papa included Dad in the world of vice. At the age of seven, Dad started smoking cigarettes bought with money he earned from Papa for driving the car across the Kansas-Missouri state line as a bootlegger! Back then, no laws stipulated a legal driving age, and who would have suspected a seven-year-old? Dad was precocious enough that I am sure he knew what the bootlegged booty tasted like.

Making money became a central focus of Dad's life. He wanted success, and worked hard for it as a child, teen, and adult. Taking on the roles of father and husband created a fierce drive to be sure he always was a good provider. I saw him sacrifice and do without so that he could not only provide for all of us, but plan ahead for unforeseen circumstances and for our college tuition. He hid stashes he referred to as "mad money," which he used as he wished. Very often that "mad money" found its way to us kids when we needed a lift in life. Dad's message, which he professed many times, remains strong with me: Always have savings for emergencies and the future.

As for my grandparents, Papa gave Mama money for her needs and household supplies. She had no money of her own. "Come, honey," she would say to me when I was little, "we buy eggs and milk." Mama would carry Papa's money in a handkerchief in one hand. Her other hand would hold on to mine, and we would go see the man with a horse-drawn cart. He brought bottles of fresh cow's milk, eggs, and produce up and down Strawberry Hill's brick streets. Something about him captivated me, like he was a character in a movie. With the clankety-clank the cart's wheels made on the brick street, I could hear the cart before I could see him. He dressed in humble, worn-out clothes, and had a big smile and a twinkle in his eyes.

On those trips, Mama's hand meant so much to me in my little world. I pass that inheritance on to my grandchildren and love to hold their little hands as we take in simple joys like walking on the railroad tracks and counting spikes. I feel our connection, and I know they feel connected to their Grandma Boom.

Every day after kindergarten, I went to Mama and Papa's house. It was my haven. I stayed there until my working parents came to pick me up. I loved walking past flowers— irises that in the spring were as big as I was—and smelling the different colors and learning their fragrances. The color lavender gave me the feeling of floating on clouds. Yellow reminded me of ladies that wore perfume in order to be noticed by men. Peach irises made me want to dance with them. And the fragrance of white irises, surely, was that of the angels.

Mama would so enjoy flowers I picked for her. "Thank you, honey," she said with a slight giggle that meant she was happy. It was fun to take flowers to my teachers, too. I wanted them to feel appreciated and special. Throughout grade school, flowers and apples were expressions of my appreciation. When I got older, I learned that I had been picking other people's flowers. I hadn't realized that I'd been stealing. When I was old enough to go to weekly confession, I did a lot of penance for flower theft to relieve my ever-present Catholic guilt.

When I was young, most of the people on Strawberry Hill were older, Mama and Papa's age. The activities of the old were sitting, standing, talking, and gossiping. Rocking chairs were popular. Lots of the old people looked mad and sad. From a young child's standpoint, getting old did not look pleasant. Not only that, but everybody looked bored. And boring. This image bothered me. I wanted older people to have fun like kids do. I never saw them do anything that resembled fun, and I didn't understand why they didn't, or maybe couldn't. Play has always expanded my experience of life and of myself, and I thought if they could play and laugh, the fun would help them feel happy. This strongly influenced my view of aging.

Play was not seen as an acceptable adult activity, and none of the older generation, be they grandparents or neighbors, freed themselves with the pleasure of playing with me or my siblings. In the end, it distanced them from me, because I could do only so much to connect with them on their level. After all, I was to be seen and not heard, and only to speak when spoken to. I felt limited around older people. Their saggy attitudes offered me no comfort or stimulation. And it made me determined that not to be saggy when I got old.

Papa seemed to have less fun than anyone. His face looked as starched as his long-sleeved white shirts. I never saw him in short sleeves, or in any color. The stiffness in his body did not invite one to sit next to him or hug him (even though hugging family was a requirement). There was no warmth. I could have hugged a plank of wood and it would have felt the same to me, rigid and cold. But I knew he loved his grandkids because both Dad and Mom said he did. I just wished he would be friendly and more fun, or even just talk to me. I never had a conversation with my grandfather.

Through the years, my observations and interactions with older people helped me to form a new image of what I wanted to be like as I aged. I didn't want to be a grandparent who sat around all day watching TV, like Papa and Mama did.

Before my grandchildren were born, I began formulating the idea that I could, as a grandparent, be more alive than ever. Having never seen that modeled, I had to discover ways to nourish my enlivening process. Before my second grandchild was born, I got two-pound weights and hiked while swinging my hands. When asked why I was doing that, I replied, "I will be holding two grandchildren at once. I want to build my strength so that I can enjoy it."

My goal was to youthen not just my body, but my spirit. Of course, it would not be the same as being twenty years old, but finding new ways to live and discover more of myself could be an adventure. I could give something uplifting to my grandchildren and share with others the opportunities that exist in growing older. Maybe my human potential would continue to develop.

So I made a deal with myself: Every new birthday, I would renew my pledge to have more fun and adventures than the year before. That excited me! I could fuel a vibrant spirit as I accumulated years. I simply had to go beyond my genetics and the environmental conditioning I had observed in my ancestors.

Papa seemed more alive when he was serving his homemade wine to neighbors. The smell of wine from the barrels in the basement of Papa and Mama's house on Strawberry Hill was quite strong, perhaps even intoxicating. When I went down the wooden steps to the barrel room and opened the hatch door, a wave of rank wine odor was released, and I had to hold my breath. At the same time, I was intrigued by the dark basement filled with smelly wooden barrels.

It was like entering the lower levels of a pirate ship. Both scary and exciting.

The hatch door to the wine cellar was in the floor. Only a few feet away was a small white table and two chairs placed under a window that faced the alley. This was post-Prohibition, so alcohol was legal, but running a bar from your back porch was not. Mrs. Lugar, Mrs. Yanokovich, and others frequently entered through the back porch door, sat at the table, and drank wine. They would leave money, which Papa would pick up off the table as he said something in Croatian to them. When I was there, they always gave me a quarter. Oh, how I loved those quarters! They felt much more substantial than dimes, nickels, and pennies. When people finished drinking, they would leave via the alley. No one ever knocked on the *front* door of the house when they wanted to come drink wine. These were the only times I saw Papa visit with others.

Money, war, and troubles

Money was a priority and a control issue. Dad had inherited Papa's stance that he should be the head of the household and in control of finances. Only instead of being submissive like Mama, Mom had a "mouth from the South." Back then, women were not seen as equal; they had roles to fulfill and were not to question. Mama simply looked down, her sadness looking like a rapidly wilting flower. Sometimes Mom's resentment about the mandates handed down to her by Dad filled the air until the mood was like a hot balloon about to burst. The dynamics in both households made me horribly uncomfortable. And I didn't like knowing that I was in for the same treatment when I got married. It felt like being doomed.

Dad loved his family, his God, his country. He had served in the Army. He transformed his own fear into courage and honor to protect what was sacred to him. Like Papa, his courage took him across an ocean and into the great unknown. He spoke of the different cultures he had encountered and the enriching experiences of his wartime travels. He was generous. Whenever he could, he gave rations to an orphanage of blind children in China. When he received orders after the war to go back to the United States, the children and nuns presented him with an embroidered silk tablecloth made by the blind children. (He left it to me because of my passion for helping children. It has always meant so much to me that both of us loved helping children.) Dad had befriended an archeologist who was on a dig in China. The archaeologist gifted Dad two vases that were unearthed as Dad watched. Rather than talk about the horrors he must have witnessed during the war, Dad focused on these highlights. The rest of it, he bottled up.

When I was growing up, Mama often asked me, "What happened to my Evo? He go to war, come back, not same. He was so sweet. Now he mad so much and shout. He mean to me." Evo was Dad's Croatian nickname. Her plea was distressing. I would try to console her, but the fact remained that her baby got a drastic makeover from the ugliness of war.

Stress management skills and self-calming techniques were not around back then. Drinking alcohol and smoking were how they relaxed. The voice of anger left by the war was like untamed cannon fodder in both homes. It exploded without warning, and left wounds with unhealed scars. I wanted to stop their pain, throw it out, make them happy so they wouldn't feel it. I could see their misery, but had no power to heal it.

Eventually I realized the pain of stress, if not redirected, causes malfunctions. Mom and Dad didn't understand why they both had bleeding ulcers. As I grew older and understood the causes behind their physical maladies, their pain led me to seek self-help tools for the prevention of ulcers and other physical ailments. My life's work would center itself around prevention and human potential.

Pipes, cigars, and cigarettes left a smoky trail that was almost always present. Papa, Dad, and Uncle Mark all relied heavily on smoking. Mom was a smoker, too. Mama was the only adult who didn't smoke. The smell attached itself to my hair and clothes, and the smoke hurt my sinuses. I felt dirty around smoke. But being a good little girl, I did not speak up. When I got a little older, I braved the smoking situation with Mom and told her the smoke odor stayed with her. She said, "NO! There is NEVER smoke odor on me." I wasn't heard.

The kitchen

On the other hand, I also grew up smelling wonderful aromas. I treasured those. Mom's meals, in her southern style of cooking, were delicious. She could cook up some "mean" meals that made our mouths water, not to mention her phenomenal desserts. Mama's dishes had comforting aromas that brought soothing sensations to my olfactory sense, taste buds, and heartstrings.

Mama taught me the secrets to making bread, and always allowed me to eat as much dough I wanted. Povetica needed pounds of walnuts. Countless times I helped Mama hand shell the walnuts. I munched on them and absorbed their aroma like I was in a big bowl of walnut stew. We worked in partial silence. Being together was comfortable and had a warm velvety feeling. We enjoyed just being in each other's company. Sometimes we talked. Always she listened.

I never felt judged by Mama. She was the only person who offered me total acceptance. With everyone else, I feared being judged or found not good enough. But in Mama's eyes, I was already perfect, so I didn't have to try. I could just be myself. She was my safe haven.

Remembering her, today I steadily maintain a non-judgmental and completely accepting attitude toward both of my grandchildren. The other day, two-year-old Kristin got into my purse, which I'd left at the front door. I said, "Kristin, I like you, but I don't like the choice you made going into my purse." Kristin looked down, not feeling good about being caught. I asked her what she wanted. "Lip chops." That is what she calls lip gloss. "I don't want you going into my purse without asking me. You can ask me for lip gloss, and I will get it for you." I got the lip gloss and handed it to her. She said, "Okay," and, with good feelings, we were on to the next thing.

Although Mom showed delight in letting us lick batter off spoons and the side of the bowl or pan, she didn't like us kids fooling around in the kitchen. She liked her space there. Both she and Mama were wonderful cooks, and from them I learned to share baked goods and invite people to meals. As for helping in the kitchen, Mama's influence has had a great impact on how I was with my children and am now with my grandchildren.

Mama's homemade egg noodles were delicious. She would make chicken noodle soup. I watched many times as she killed the chicken by wringing its neck. Sometimes it would keep running around. I thought it was coming after me. It was scary, but I grew to like the challenge of outrunning it. Mama would put chicken feet in the soup. Countless times we kids fought over the chicken feet. Dad taught us to suck out the very sweet, tender meet in between the toes and joints. There wasn't much there, but it was worth working for. It tickled Mama that we enjoyed her food so much. She giggled at our chicken feet fights. I also understood that no part of the chicken was wasted.

Uncle Mark and Aunt Kay

Uncle Mark and Aunt Kay lived with Mama and Papa their entire lives, with one exception—when Uncle Mark was briefly married to Harriet, an alcoholic whom he divorced shortly after the marriage. Aunt Kay's boyfriend was killed in World War II. She became an alcoholic. I discovered this when her coat, hanging in a closet, banged against the door when I opened it. Bottles of alcohol were sewn into pockets along the hem. Our family was saturated in alcohol.

Uncle Mark had a spark, and he was much more involved with all of us children than the other adults. When Mama, Papa, Aunt Kay, and he moved near us in Miros Circle, he took us to school many mornings. To make the ten-mile drive fun, he always had a rhyme or song for us. One of his favorites was, "Mares eat oats and does eat oats and little lambs eat ivy. A kid will eat ivy, too, wouldn't you?" We kids were expected to respond, or he would keep repeating it.

The air around Uncle Mark was calmer than that around Dad. He was a different kind of male role model. He connected with us kids. I had struggled to feel good about myself, and Uncle Mark sprinkled doses of nourishment for my spirit by talking with me. He helped me build my confidence because he let me see that I was important to him. He became my confidante. He also bought me special things that my parents could not afford. I still have a vanity he bought me when I was eleven. And I will never forget that fake fur coat we shopped for when I wanted to feel like a movie star.

"Be silly. Be honest.
Be kind."

~ RALPH WALDO EMERSON

"Loving kindness is the most powerful force in the universe. Having true empathy is to understand another's pain and suffering from a place of power. Your job is to also create new possibilities."

~ KUAN YIN

CHAPTER 3

Unforgettable Childhood Memories

The Flood of '51

Throughout the years, I have learned that the memory of a trauma feels more alive because of the intensity registered in the emotional body and in the brain's chemistry. The flood of 1951 in the Argentine district of Kansas City is one of those memories for me. I was two. My brother Ted was a baby.

I can still feel how tightly I held on to Mom's hand, and remember looking up at her as she looked out from the hill where we lived. The world smelled dank. I looked at baby Ted, wrapped in a blanket and sleeping on Mom's shoulder. Below us, we watched the fast running floodwaters and the remnants of life and death tumbling in it. A rooftop rushed past a tree. Then a dead cow swiftly passed the shore, swirling once as its body hit something in the water. I was too young to understand. But I remember the images. And the fear. And the safety of holding Mom's hand. As I grew older and became a mom, then a grandmom, I wanted my hand to signify a safe haven for the children. Mom and Mama reinforced that decision with their loving hands.

Difficulties in childhood

What I know now is that my frequent and severe illnesses as a child brought comfort, not just because I was cared for, but because Mom and Dad would get along. They worked together well in crisis. When my siblings or I were sick, they stopped fighting.

I work with healing energy, and I have observed that it is natural to absorb others' stress, tension, emotions, negativity, or positivity. My parents were not happy and fought a lot. I absorbed that energy, and it made me sick. They didn't realize it, nor did I. They would not have chosen to make any of their children sick. They had good intentions, were good folks, and loved us in the best way they could. But energy is energy. In our 3-D world, we don't pay attention to it because we don't see it.

When Dad or Mom called me "stupid" for doing something wrong or not figuring something out, I felt sick to my stomach. Hearing "stupid idiot" felt even worse, like something was caving in on my heart, squishing my stomach, and pushing my head downward. They were trying to get a message into my "thick skull." Frequent and sometimes serious illnesses, coupled with being told I was less than smart, provoked both self-doubt and self-pity in me. As my path brought me lessons that showed me how to pull in the reins on those energy suckers if I didn't want to drown in depression, they became two powerful teachers on my journey to self-actualization.

For a time, self-doubt and self-pity, the two ugly little culprits, devoured me like a house being sucked into a sinkhole. Self-doubt created the feeling of a musty cloud descending upon me and mud pouring into my being. Self-pity chewed me up and spat me out like a used-up dishrag. Both caused me to underrate myself, and rendered me useless and hopeless. Poor me. Being sick and abused, there was room for self-pity and self-doubt to anchor inside me, as ignorance and fear urged me to rent them space in my body.

It took many decades for me to heal. I didn't have a killer spray for these core pillagers of my self-worth. Oddly enough, it has been the major crises that have pushed me to the limits of what I thought I could manage. Crisis has proven itself a catalyst for change. And getting older has brought wisdom as salve to my wounds, some of which were self-inflicted. I discovered that storms of our inner world do come with rainbows. I keep moving forward, onward, upward, and trustward on a journey that, on an emotional scale, has registered as *tumultuous*.

Survival instinct

"I'm going to kill you!" Dad's voice would boom out in anger at Mom. She would retaliate, "Not if I kill you first!" Every time I heard these shouts, I wanted God to come down from heaven and save us. Fear became a tidal wave of body knots tangling inside my stomach. My most profound fear was that my parents would kill each other during their knock-down-drag-out fights. (That was their description of what occurred. They didn't actually knock down and drag out.)

Many times, we kids were told to stay away from their closet. Mom and Dad kept a loaded gun in there. As they fought, their blood curdling screaming, cussing, and death threats sent a flurry of thoughts and feelings through me like a raging storm. I desperately wanted to hide the gun, but out of fear of mishandling it, I never acted on it. I began to hate guns; they represented a living threat to my well-being if my parents killed each other.

As the oldest of four, my concern was keeping my siblings safe. I would gather them and lead them either into the back bedroom or upstairs. Then I shut the door and tried to keep them engaged. I wanted to draw their focus away from our parents' storm.

Mom and Dad were well matched in their cussing and screaming. During their ferocious battles, a faint little voice would arise in me: *There has to be another way to live.* My whole body felt like it had been bound in chains. Children find survival tools. I developed nervous habits and became sick. Other survival tools are withdrawal, hyperactivity, eating or not eating, sleep disorders, nightmares, escaping into a daydream world—whatever a child's mind can, consciously or not, develop to cope. After a blowout, to escape the dark tension, I went either to the basement or outside to play. Playing let me be in control of creating a different life, one where all good things were possible. Dress-ups and fun thoughts gave me release and soothed me. They always allowed me to create my own delightful reality.

In our household, children were not allowed to have opinions. The operative theme was children should be seen and not heard. In our family, Dad was the mind and Mom was the emotional body. They didn't know how to teach us to pay attention to our own thoughts and feelings, or how to manage them effectively, only that we should repress them. In that sense, I felt like a caged animal, not allowed to be free and fend for myself. Mom and Dad had not learned coping and communication skills, so they could not teach us by example. It was so confusing when Dad would insist we children should "Do what I say, not what I do." When I was older, I figured out that he simply wanted more for us than what he experienced in life. But that didn't register in the mind of a child, and I grew up thinking if my opinion didn't matter, then *I* didn't matter.

On a TV show, I heard about Native American pow-wows where everyone got to talk. When I babysat my brothers and sister, I started talking with them, asking them what they thought about whatever was going on in our lives. I wanted us to find our voices. But it wasn't until I had kids of my own that I started the practice of having a family meeting. We tried to make sure everyone was heard and questions and feelings were addressed. I wanted my kids to grow up knowing they counted. Now, with my grandkids, I invite them to drum on a large drum to get their feelings out first, then we talk. Even when my children and grandchildren were tiny babies, I explained things and asked their opinions. Holding one of my little ones, I would say something like, "It's a nice day outside. Do you think it's a good idea to go outside and play in the pretty leaves?" Even if they didn't answer, they always connected with my eye contact. I knew they could feel the tone of my voice.

For me, living in the past was too painful. I felt like a victim. I wanted power, and the urge to use the past as an instrument of transformation became irresistible. As I looked back so I could uncover my feelings about my family, about events, and about what it all meant to me, my learning began in morsels. I came to reframe the past, to see it as a curriculum for what I needed to learn about who I am, so I could be true to that. My rich inner world has made me happy. Eventually, my sister, Karen, worked with this thread of awareness as well. As for our brothers, Ted and Johnny, at a young age the family tension spun them into finding ways to alter their reality through substance abuse.

Mom and Dad did not know ways other than the ones they grew up with. I wish I could have helped them, and helped myself as I was growing up. But the information just wasn't there for us. Now, Grandma Boom teaches preschool age children and my grandchildren about feelings, body connections to thoughts and feelings, and how to do deep breathing. I encourage them to recognize, appreciate, and develop their rich inner world in ways that are healthy, natural, and fun. And I am passionate about stimulating communication and preventing emotional trauma. This is all a gift from what my parents did not know.

Punishment

For punishment, sometimes we were grounded. Sometimes we had to stay in our rooms for a certain length of time. Sometimes a toy was taken away. While these were not pleasant, they were better than the physical punishments. Mom's favorite was the peach tree switch.

We had a peach tree in the backyard. Knowing what was coming, it was torturous waiting for her to go break a switch off the tree. The most embarrassing time to be whipped with a peach tree switch was summertime. If I got called out for smart mouthing, I'd have to pull down my pants, and Mom would raise her arm, hand up over her shoulder to get a good momentum, and haul off. The most painful was when she struck my bare bottom at an angle and the strike also hit my legs. A welt rose up, and it always bled. Wearing shorts in the summertime and exposing the welt meant all the neighbors would see that I had been a bad girl. So not only did it sting, and not only did it trigger me having terrible thoughts about myself, I was also mortified. My spirit was crushed.

If Mom was too busy to go get a peach tree switch, she grabbed the fly swatter hanging on the side of the refrigerator. It stung and left an imprint, but it never made me bleed. But the idea of getting fly guts on me was awful.

The thick leather belt Dad wore to keep his pants up was a painfully harsh implement of punishment. Only Dad used it. He would take whoever had transgressed into the back bedroom, pants were taken down, and the leather belt would slash across bare bottom and legs. When this happened to me, I felt like an animal that had to be beaten in order to be tamed. I lost any sense of goodness about myself. Sometimes I found myself wishing I could be perfect; then I would not have to be beaten.

When I was still a child, I decided that when I had my own babies I would not hit them. Some part of me knew there had to be another way. I practiced talking to my baby-dolls about their imaginary dealings that got them in trouble.

My parents did not consider physical punishment to be abuse. They just wanted to make sure we were "good kids." Still, if Mom or Dad was upset about something else, the physical punishment was harsher and hurt more. Even if they were not aware of it, it served as a release for them. Eventually, I grew to honor my parents' good intentions and to have compassion for their pain and struggles, but their punishments were abusive. And demoralizing. I have had to work hard to fix the impact it had on my self-worth. Inside me, the voice was steady: Break the cycle. I have been successful in doing that with my own family.

The art and saving grace of dress-ups

Dress-up was the heaven-sent foundation for my play. Still is. Imagining scenarios with other kids clicked us into timelessness. I longed to put dress-ups on my parents and grandparents so we could play and laugh together. I often wonder what they would have been like as children to play with, or even as adults.

Mom sometimes played jacks with us on the kitchen floor, or Monopoly. Her most delightful play was when she chased us and our friends around and outside the house with the fly swatter, acting like she was going to swat us. Our screams of delight filled the air. Dad, on very rare occasions, played checkers, Chinese checkers, or catch with a softball. But creative play was not in their range of play. I can't help but think that they would have been so cute in dress-ups.

Dress-ups allowed me to discover and act out many issues in creative play. I always have a variety of dress-ups for my grandchildren. I did the same for my children. Two days ago, my inner child was twirling around with streamers, joining my grandkiddos in a song and dance we created together. It wasn't harmonious, but it was great fun. We were wearing different color wigs, connecting in a joyful creative space.

Many years ago, I adopted a philosophy shared with me by a woman who attended one of my workshops. She complimented me on my clothes. She told me that she looked at clothing from an artistic standpoint and felt it is our responsibility to decorate the world. *Bingo!* That struck a chord with me. Dress-ups allow me freedom, color, and artistic expression. Most of all, it makes every day fun to get up and get dressed.

What I found in dress-ups and creative play was that I could explore the many parts of myself. I love shiny things, sparkles, bright colors—all the opposite of my school uniforms. Most of all, I felt excited by my fresh perceptions of myself. In being free to be me, I feel more alive. I don't fit into the norm. For my entire life, various people have tried to control me, to squish me into some stifling persona. I have grown weary of caring about being accepted. In her own way, Mom got to that same place, and as I continue to play in my dress-ups, I have adopted her sentiment: *I don't give a rat's ass what anybody thinks!*

Life-giving imagination

On rare occasions, Dad would go outside with us kids in the summer when it was dark and we would lie on the sidewalk or the front lawn and look at the sky. Dad's thoughts would meander to UFO talk and other mysterious subjects. Together, we used imaginations to stretch. How wonderfully satisfying to connect without everyday distractions. And I felt safe, away from anger's tentacles. This was a kind of "play" Dad could engage in.

When I was little, I longed to feel emotional closeness to Dad. Tidbits of it sprinkled my childhood. In his own way, he tried. I could feel his strength, and that he was dedicated to being a good dad. To play with him was a special treat that, for a time, soothed my longing for closeness. When we linked our minds with imagination, it felt like we were allied equals.

Einstein said, "Imagination is more important than knowledge." When I first heard that from Dad, I was too young to understand what it meant. Dad followed that up with, "If it is possible in the mind, it *is* possible." It took time and more maturity before I grasped what he meant. These inspirational statements proved to be critical to my ability to open to my own human potential.

When she was relaxed, Mom could use her imagination and let the little girl inside her be expressed. One of my favorite memories is riding the waves with her at Daytona Beach. We were rodeo gals in the Wild West on those waves.

After her breast cancer and mastectomy in the early 1970s, I wondered if she would heal psychologically. Several years after her surgery, I got my answer. The funniest thing she ever did was squirt me at the beach with her bra filler. I loved that she took a serious concern that had felt devastating to her and managed to come to a place of humor with it. *That* is successful healing.

When my grandson, Jackson, was three years old, we went on a walk. He directed me to lie down face up on a public sidewalk. There we were, sixty years different in age, staring up at the sky. Dots of fluffy-puffy marshmallow clouds and a brilliant blue backdrop blessed our eyes. (Thank the gods for sunglasses.) Jackson let his arms float above him. Several times his hands grasped something in mid-air, then he pulled his hands down to his face. He directed me to do the same. I asked why. He shared the secret for having the cleanest faces on earth—cloud washing. There we were, Grandma Boom and Jackson, lying on a public sidewalk, pulling glorious marshmallow clouds down to our faces to get cleaned up. We were there together, in a world where anything was possible. This one is permanently etched in my heart.

Now when I am with my grandchildren, the inner child in me as grandparent is enlivened. When Jackson crawled, I crawled. We explored under table territories and chased each other around chairs. Sure, it was hard on my knees, but I healed them with homeopathic medicine. When my granddaughter, Kristin, began to crawl, I was smarter and got knee pads, two pairs for double the protection! So, no more knee damage, just amazing experiences with both grandchildren in their world. When I enter their world, I feel a strong bond with them, and our relationships are sealed with kisses, hugs, and the boatload of fun we continually create together in play, our colorful relationship glue.

Family first, prayers, and meals

"Kiss your dad goodnight." It was a family rule that we had to kiss our parents goodnight. When we had had a falling out with them, it wasn't easy, but the theme of family love was nourished. More than once Dad said, "Blood is thicker than water." Then he would explain, saying that there was nothing more important than family and we were to do more for family than anyone else. Even if one of our siblings committed murder, it was our responsibility to stick by that person. Today, I retain this value of putting family first, but I do not force kissing and hugging.

Prayer was a regular part of our life. Mealtime prayers gave us kids the opportunity to see who could recite the long, one-sentence Catholic pre-meal blessing the fastest. My brother Ted could recite it like he was on fire and running for water. I didn't feel gratitude though, even when Dad told us about the starving children he had seen in WWII.

Nighttime prayers were on the knees by the bedside, and silent. I would say a couple of formal prayers, like the Our

Father and Hail Mary, sometimes the Glory Be, then make requests: *Please, God, don't let my Mom and Dad kill each other. Keep them safe. Maybe you could make them happy, maybe they wouldn't be so upset. Please send some extra angels to watch over them. Thanks, God. Amen.*

At our house, we were expected to all eat together. Meals were family together time. Supper was always served at 6:00 p.m. If anyone was late, he or she was punished with an extra chore, missing a TV show, or going to bed early. If Mom and Dad were in a prolonged state of disagreement, they would ask us kids to ask the other parent to pass the mashed potatoes. I maintained my focus on the food in front of me– the taste, smells, textures—and chewed ever so slowly. It was how I survived the tension at the table. When I smelled the food being passed around in bowls, I got in trouble for smelling it. I was scolded for chewing Jell-O. Even so, humorous moments happened as well. Dad would belch or fart, and Mom would make a disgusted face, and we kids laughed. Dad insisted he was paying a compliment to her cooking, which always threw Mom into a tizzy.

Children were not considered equal to adults

Over and over we were told to mind our manners and keep our places as children. If we had company, unless it was suggested we go play in another room, we were to sit quietly and listen. Unless it was an emergency, we were not to interrupt, ever. Sometimes my sister or I got in trouble when we interrupted because one of our brothers hit us. We considered that an emergency. I appreciate the role of manners in life, that they show respect, but I didn't like feeling less than whole.

When something upsetting happened, Dad's normal comment often was, "Don't wear your feelings on your sleeves." The first time I heard it, I looked at my sleeves for my feelings. I finally figured out it meant two things: don't be emotional and don't take it personally. Being a sensitive child, I was guilty of both. Feelings would swell up, and I had to contain them. I'm sure it fueled my illnesses. I could feel so strongly, yet those feelings were trapped inside. Instinctively, I knew we needed to express what was inside us and be heard, but I wasn't sure how to go about it. I started to encourage my siblings to talk about their feelings, with limited results. Mom was a better listener when the situation was emotional. That is, when she could. Sometimes she was overwhelmed with her own intense emotions. Dad used yelling, cussing, reprimands, arguing, and stomping to release his emotions. His opinions were strong and not to be questioned. Mom cussed and blurted out some of her Southern sayings. The one no one wanted to hear was, "You better give your soul to God, because your ass is mine!" It often felt like the family was a powder keg about to blow. We needed healthy releases, but didn't have them.

When Mom or Dad offered encouragement, it refreshed me like a waterfall on a hot day. I felt more alive. I could see myself and my potential through someone else's eyes more clearly than through my own eyes, which were clouded with self-doubt. Mom was better at it than Dad, although he did become a more encouraging communicator with us kids when we got older.

Over time, I learned healthy, creative ways to release feelings, and now when I have feelings that could bog me down, I make sure to release them. Deep breathing and exercise are my first go-tos. I have a dammit doll that I can hit, and in no time at all, I wind up laughing at myself. Meditating is great, but sometimes I need the physical release that does no harm. I have a Bozo the Clown punching bag that takes the hit, then pops back up. Actually, it looks like Bozo enjoys it. When they are full of emotion, I invite my grandchildren to bop Bozo. I have also shown them how to release feelings with art, to let go of anger by stomping on bubbles, and other safe tactics we develop on the fly.

As for encouragement ("Oh, Kristin, that was so sweet of you to hug Jackson when he fell." "Jackson, you are so kind to your sister to get her jacket for her. Thank you."), not only does it benefit the children, but I feel terrific. It feels good to plant seeds of confidence and self-worth in my little grand-ones. I know it fuels a sense of their goodness and potential. These kids receive the nourishment of encouragement from their parents, me and other relatives.

When I was a child and others were ill, it had a deep impact on my psyche. I wanted to help care for them. As a toddler, I gave humble little massages. Sitting at Mom's feet and rubbing them through all her pregnancies or when she was tired became a regular ritual. Rubbing Dad's feet, shoulders, and back were a small token of my love and gratitude for all his hard work. I gave my brothers and sister rubs when they were upset or ill. A common response to my offerings became, "You have magic hands." People always reported feeling better.

One of my hobbies became a search for healing tools from other times, other cultures, other philosophies. One of my favorites at this life stage is using tuning forks. Considered "sound acupuncture," they bring amazing inner peace. It makes sense to me that if we can tune musical instruments, we should be able to tune ourselves. When I give people the magic of tuning forks, they give it rave reviews.

Starting kindergarten

Kindergarten was a new world, one without parents or relatives. Mom and Dad stood outside the kindergarten door and watched as I took my place in the back of the room, two-thirds of the way along the row. Then the nun closed the door. The sound of the door shutting stiffened everyone in the room. Dead silence. Fear shook me like a leaf, and it was all I could do not to wail.

Then Sister Proxeda spoke. Even though her voice was unfamiliar, it was kind. "Children, take out your crayons." Although she was small, she had a strong voice, and we rummaged through the new school supplies in our desks, pulled out crayons, and began to color. All those open boxes of Crayolas emitted a memorable aroma, like the crayons were cooking.

The olfactory sense intrigues me. Knowing it to be the oldest active sense in humans, I use it to create effects. One day I took some dried lavender and had my grandchildren smell it. I asked how they liked it. Both said it smelled good. I told them that when I make a good choice with my behavior, if I could smell it, the good choice would smell like lavender. Later, I directed Jackson to get out his bad feelings with some play dough. When he finished, he showed me the green glob and reported he felt better, but he was holding his nose. When I asked him why, he said, "Grandma Boom, bad feelings smell really bad."

The bathroom rule

In kindergarten, I learned I had to make it on my own in a new world. I found it shocking that I had to go public with what had always been a private matter. Sister Proxeda explained the bathroom rule at St. John the Baptist School: If we had to go Number One, we were to raise a hand with one finger up in the air. If we had to go Number Two, we were to raise a hand and put two fingers up. And if we raised one finger and were gone too long, someone would come to bring us back and we would be in big doo-doo for lying about our bathroom needs. I figured the rule came directly from God through the nuns and it was not to be disputed.

When I told Mom about it, her "Oh Lorda Mercy!" summed it up for both of us. It was nothing short of horrifying to imagine a room full of people knowing if I had to pee or poop. I had been a "frequent flyer" to the bathroom, but I hoped never to have to go to the bathroom at school. Ever. One poor girl who sat near me was terribly shy and she wet her pants every day. She never raised her hand. I understood. But it was hard to be near her because she smelled. At home I began reporting to my parents and siblings when I had to go to the bathroom. It became a habit in life. I still announce it.

Recently, my two-year-old granddaughter, Kristin, was holding my hand at a restaurant on our way to the bathroom.

She stopped at the table of young, pregnant, professional looking woman who was quietly eating. Kristin looked at her and declared, "I am Kristin. I have pink toesies. And I have to go poop!" Oh god, did the bathroom rule become part of my DNA and pass on to her? The woman opened her eyes wide, kind of smiled, then looked at me like I surely had something to say. All I could muster was, "They're so innocent and *honest* at this age!"

Labeling private parts

All families have their preferences with private part labeling. My family was no different. However, the choice proved to be, well, a problem for me once I entered grade school. I didn't know the anatomical names of anything on my body until fifth grade. School friends educated me. Till then, I went by what Mom taught us. Regardless of gender, everything below the belt was referred to as our "sunshine." I've no idea how that name came about.

In first grade we learned the song, "You are my sunshine, my only sunshine..." I thought I was going to die. At home everything was so private and hush-hush. At school it seemed everyone knew everything and we were even singing about our private parts. As we learned the song, my face was burning with embarrassment. Even my eyes felt hot. It was a confusing time for me. Stoic nuns with everything hidden except hands and faces, rules forbade talking with the opposite sex, sharing publicly what we were going to do in the bathroom was the norm. And singing about our private parts, well, that was the biggest shock of my young life.

They called me "Little Mother"

Mothering is my nature. Or perhaps it should be referred to as nurturing when I am not in Mom or Grandma Boom mode. It started long ago when my brother Ted was born eighteen months after I was. When I was older, Mom told me Dad would not even go to the hospital to see her and the new baby. A friend of Dad's, Paul, climbed the hospital wall and entered through the window, since only relatives were permitted to visit. He knew Dad wasn't coming to visit, and he brought Mom flowers. This always struck me as odd because Dad wanted twelve children, an idea Mom regarded as abhorrent.

Evidently, as soon as Ted came home, I began to dote on him. They say he didn't speak until he was two because I knew what he wanted and would speak for him. "Teddy is thirsty," and "Teddy has to go potty." Mom said that when I was two, they began to call me "Little Mother."

As it turned out, Dad and Ted never did hit it off. I could feel Ted's sadness, which brought sadness to me. I could feel the hurt in his heart physically in mine. There was nothing I could do to change the fights that Ted and Dad had, nor the feeling between Mom and Dad about Ted. All I could do was love him and take care of him. He was troubled. I have always had a natural tendency to help troubled children.

Moving from Ann Avenue to a new life in the country

For about a year we lived on Strawberry Hill, up the hill from Mama and Papa's house. Then we moved to Miros

Circle, ten miles away. The shape of the roads in Miros Circle felt like a big hug to me. Our brick house was at the bottom of the circle. Two roads going uphill were on either side. We referred to the one on the left as the Crilly Hill, after our neighbors the Crillys, and the one on the right as the Sormanti Hill, after our neighbors the Sormnatis. The warmth and closeness of neighbors embraced us in that Miros Circle hug. People watched out for one another's' kids and helped out in emergencies. In storms and power outages, sharing food and concern for everyone's welfare were priceless attributes that gave our neighborhood the feel of a small village where we were safe.

It was a high point for Mom and Dad to be homeowners of the new brick house in a rural area. It felt like a wonderful new life with more space inside and outside, and a farm behind our property. Hearing cows moo was such a delight. Mom and Dad could provide better for their growing family. We even got pets.

Maja was a Chihuahua. That puppy filled our days with wonders. Playing with this furry being, talking to him, watching him, inviting him to be with us in our fantasy playtimes. Maja communicated with me in his own way. We understood each other.

One day, Maja wasn't in the basement. I couldn't find him anywhere, and I was beside myself. Mom and Dad said he was just "gone." It didn't make sense. I never did learn what happened to him, and I stressed terribly for ages. If he had died, I wish they would have told me so at least there could have been closure.

Soon life got exciting, as Mom's sister and her family moved in with us for a while because they were having financial difficulties. I loved having more playmates!

During that time, Ted was sick, and I saw Mom doing something I didn't understand. She explained that she was giving him an enema so he would feel better. Always wanting to help others, that afternoon, when I was playing in the basement with my younger female cousin, I thought it would be great to help her feel better, too. So I had her pull her pants down and I started poking at her bottom with a stick.

Mom happened to come down to get laundry and saw me. "Janice Carolyn! What *are* you doing? Get that stick away from her bottom!" I tried to explain that I wanted to help my cousin feel better like Mom helped Ted, but she wouldn't hear of it. I got a spanking, which confused me to no end. And my aunt would not let her daughter near me for a couple of days. It was years before I figured out why they were upset.

In later adult years, when working with children in creative therapeutic situations, with my own children growing up, and now my grandchildren, I make it a point to explain the *why* of things. Then I check to see if they have grasped the concept. The basement "enema" attempt left me with a strong conviction of the need to explain why.

When Karen was born

We called my maternal grandmother Big Mama, so as not to confuse her with Mama, my other grandmother. One day Mom said, "Big Mama is coming to stay with us. She loves you and Ted. When she comes, you mind your manners." Big Mama, Ida Harrison, had an austere coldness about her. She had raised Mom as a strict Southern Baptist—no dancing, no playing cards, and many other rules. My grandfather, Oscar Lee Harrison, had been the town mayor and minister of the Baptist Church in Wildwood, Florida, before he was killed by a train where he worked. I never saw Big Mama laugh. Even though Mom said Big Mama loved us, I couldn't feel the warmth of love, not like my other grandmother.

The morning Karen was born, I was standing in the hallway looking through the window when Big Mama approached me and said, "You have a baby sister." I was so excited! I remember thinking that I knew the baby was a girl and that she was supposed to come to our family. It wasn't clear to me why I thought that. I just thought it. I knew she was going to be my baby-doll. From the first day home, she was in my care a great deal, even though I was just six. After all, I was "Little Mother."

It had been hard to wait for Karen to arrive. I didn't understand why Mom had to go to a hospital. It seemed to me it would be much more efficient for the stork to deliver the baby at home instead of having to land on the roof of the hospital. I believed in the stork until the sixth grade, when classmates informed me how babies were born.

Johnny's birth

I was twelve when Johnny was born. One evening in the beginning of the pregnancy, I overheard Mom telling Dad she did not want to be pregnant. Dad could not condone an abortion. They haggled back and forth. Finally, Mom agreed to keep the baby if she could have all new maternity clothes. Dad's arm was twisted. He agreed. As with Ted and Karen, Johnny became one of my wards. I felt sorry for him having to lie in bed so much, so I would take him out. Loving babies and children always brought happiness to me.

From the time he was very small, Johnny was cute and mischievous. He loved to tease. When I began dating, his favorite thing was to hide my shoes so I couldn't leave with my date until I found them. Sometimes I wanted to clobber him, but he was so cute and funny that I always wound up laughing.

Karen and Johnny got to spend more time with Mama and Papa than I did. Mom had taken a full-time job at Procter and Gamble. So before they entered kindergarten, Karen and Johnny stayed at Mama and Papa's when Mom worked. (It was Mama who took care of them. Papa didn't babysit.)

On Miros Circle we had many friends in the neighborhood of all ages, and often they were in our home. On weekends and holidays, we considered our house Grand Central Station. Miros Circle was an amazing, wonderful neighborhood, and for many years we were part of a small community. Everyone looked out for one another's kids. In the mornings, women had coffee while still in their rollers, and sometimes even in their pajamas. Barbecues became regular events. And neighbors helped out when there was sickness, celebrated life triumphs, supported one another in crisis and death. It was a time when there were no thefts in this working class neighborhood. People trusted one another.

The Sormantis, the Crillys, the Zawatskis, the Mizells, the

Stallards, and the Benders were but a few of the families that were a solid part of my childhood in this close-knit neighborhood. The Zawatskis and Crillys had the best basements for us to put on fun plays, dance, play games, and have meetings. The Sormantis had a back porch on which one could fry an egg from the sun's reflection on a hot day, as their oldest son, Raymond, demonstrated one summer. The Mizells had the best Christmas decorations on top of their house. The Stallards got the first riding lawn mower in the neighborhood that triggered a chain reaction. The Benders hired me to babysit, as did Stallards.

"EEEEEAWKEEEEE" I would call out the upstairs window in warm weather. It was a signal Linda Sormanti, my neighbor two doors down, and we used our "call" instead of phoning to see if the other could come out and play. When I yelled like that, I felt like Tarzan. Linda was darling in so many ways. I envied her freckles. During our teenage years, she led the way with her stories about dating and boys.

The Benders lived next-door to us. The parents, Larry and Bev, were my sister's godparents. They gave me a statue of the Blessed Virgin that I always took to the basement during tornado warnings. Some nights, Dad and Larry went "froggin" at some ponds. Beer accompanied them, and they brought back a batch of frogs and stories. Mom would cook up the frog legs, which tasted sweeter than fried chicken.

Larry Bender would drive up a hill, then take off, as Mom would say, bat-shit crazy-fast. We kids would stand on the back seat, our stomachs doing flip-flops, and yell "Wheeeeeeeeeeeeeeee." I still think of Larry when I create my own form of "Wheeeeeeeeeeeeee" on hills and passing on the fun to my grandies. My form is tamer than his, though. And every time, I say, "Thank you, Larry Bender, for adding to my life fun that has lasted sixty years!" How refreshing that an adult had fun with us kids. His inner child was present and accounted for.

"Jimmy, get that blasted sand out of your mouth and stop swallowing it." The Stallards' driveway adjoined ours. Often Ethel, with a cup of cowboy coffee in her hand, called out to her son, a persistent sand-eater. Her husband, Dal, worked as a DJ at a radio station and gave me new records. Memories of dancing to the new tunes such as "Spanish Harlem" are still with me.

Not understanding me

When I was a young child, before I went to school, it felt like pieces to the puzzle of me were missing. I had out-of-the-ordinary experiences that I didn't know how to relate or explain. When I did manage to share them with my parents, they would look away, leaving me baffled, confused, and wondering what was wrong with me. Now I can see they simply didn't know how to handle my experiences. They, too, were baffled.

For example, when I was four, I was getting something from the bedroom I shared with my brother. Suddenly, from a stooped position, I bolted upright—I heard a voice and had a vision. It was showing me something, and the voice said: *Everyone is a dot in God's tummy.* The truth of this came as indisputable.

Many other times, I heard whole conversations before they happened, especially ones between my parents. I heard the conversations in my mind, then a moment or two later I heard them for real. I shared this with Mom and Dad, but they looked away from me and left the room. They did not even acknowledge I had spoken. They probably thought I was fibbing.

I know now that my parents had their own intuitive experiences. It was common to hear Mom say something akin to "I've got a feeling something isn't right about that situation." Or to say with a furrowed brow, "Something just isn't right. I've got that feeling." Dad, on the other hand, would never say he had a feeling but would strongly pronounce, "My gut instinct says..." or very commonly, "I've got a hunch that..." They never used the word "intuition," but they were using theirs. It confirms for me that intuition was present in our lives.

I wish they had recognized that their intuition, by way of hunches and feelings, and the experiences I had were kindred. I hated not being heard. I was trying to find my way, and not being heard was disconcerting and discouraging. I did not feel respected as a person and would get a bad feeling about myself, like I was a piece of nothing. This is why I am resolute about listening to my children and grandchildren and responding to them.

Did I really come from Mars?

After a number of such extraordinary experiences, Mom started to joke that I was from Mars. When I was a preschooler, that just meant some shiny star up in the sky was my real home. Throughout my childhood I also heard "sounds." The sounds were all a high pitch inside my head. I was not a victim of ear infections. I asked others if they heard sounds like that. Nope. A girlfriend said maybe I was hearing things that animals hear, that are inaudible to "normal" humans. When I would mention it to Mom, she would laugh and insist I was from Mars.

I came to take her opinion as truth, and figured the sounds must be the Martian language and my Martian friends were sending me messages. So I would stop what I was doing and listen more intently. Even though I could not understand any literal meaning from my Martian friends, it became a comfort to know they were sending me messages. Then I began to wonder if they were the ones telling me about the conversations I heard before they happened. Maybe, I thought, they were responsible for all the other strange occurrences. And sometimes, I thought it was angels.

Through the years, people have suggested I am hearing my inner world—perhaps my chakras, the body's energy centers. But I still think of Martians.

Eventually, I came to understand that what was happening to me was normal in terms of human potential. If Einstein used only fifteen percent of his brain, that means to me that we all have untold potential for development. When I discovered that, like animal instinct, intuition is a natural part of the brain's functioning, something clicked for me. I no longer told myself I was crazy. What a relief to finally see that I was normal and just tapping more of my own human potential, parts that others may not understand.

Learning: A treat, but incomplete

I find learning new things exciting, empowering, expansive. To me, it is an adventure, a challenge, something to play with, and in the end, an accomplishment. As a young child, learning the ABCs was nothing short of magic. Singing them was a joy, and it brought on an urge to dance them. Nix that in school, though, where there was only one way to learn and you either comprehended it or didn't. No extra help. No personalized guidance to fit your learning style. I would have loved schooling that allowed whole-body learning. Dancing to the alphabet at school would have been another manifestation of heaven on earth. I didn't have whole-body learning when young, but I can facilitate it now. Now, when my grandson sings the ABCs, he drums, he dances, and he acts out the letters.

Forty years ago, I discovered that learning in 3-D accelerates the absorption and retention of information. Seeing that memorizing something is not as effective as learning it hands-on, I create tactile tools. For example, to teach children not to lie, I made an aluminum foil ball and stuck half-toothpicks into it. It looks like a rough model of Sputnik and is prickly to hold. When Jackson had chocolate pudding on his face but denied he had eaten any, I took him to the mirror and showed him the smatterings on his face. Then I had him hold the prickly aluminum foil lie-ball and explained that this was what a lie looks like and feels like inside the body. I asked him to show me where he felt the lie inside himself. He pointed to his tummy. He looked at the lie-ball in his hand and said, "This doesn't feel very good, Grandma

Boom." I said, "No it doesn't. A lie doesn't feel good staying inside your tummy." He handed the lie-ball back to me and started telling me about other lies he had told recently. He learned for himself with 3-D learning.

Grade school uniforms and equality ... NOT

"Time to get measured for your school uniform." It was an unwelcome directive. In kindergarten, I wore regular clothes, but grades one through ten required uniforms. Ugly uniforms. The required attire for grade school girls was: navy blue jumper, navy blue cardigan, white blouse, and a blue beanie to wear in church. It was aggravating to the girls that the boys got to wear what they wanted, except for jeans. We girls could not wear patent leather shoes because they might show a reflection of what was underneath our uniform jumpers.

We were taught at school that uniforms produced an atmosphere of equality. I knew that was hogwash. Discrimination was alive and well. We were discriminated against by some of the teachers and the other children's parents because my mother was a Southern Baptist and had been divorced.

Getting in trouble at school was threatening. If someone was really unruly, or skipped school without a good reason, the police were called. That was terrifying. My siblings and I never experienced it firsthand, but we saw police officers returning children to school as well as taking them away. I cannot imagine the punishment my parents would have delivered if I had done something to warrant a ride with a police officer. Fear certainly kept me in line.

Every morning before school, students were required to attend church. This meant we fasted and received Communion and ate the host that was the body of Jesus Christ. It dissolved on the tongue, and my hunger made it taste better than marshmallows. Plus, Jesus joined with me. Then we got to have breakfast in the cafeteria. Including Sundays, I attended Mass six times a week. My bony knees felt it.

Classrooms were divided into a girl section and a boy section, as was the playground. Girls and boys were not to talk to each other. Having two brothers, it was odd for me not to be allowed to talk to boys, especially since we did after school anyway.

One day, the girls were playing sock ball (we made balls from old socks), and the ball went on the boys' side of the playground. So I asked a boy to give us our ball. Sister Claudia, the principal, saw me. I had to spend the next recess inside as punishment. If only the nuns had realized that making boys forbidden fruit made them more interesting! As a mom and grandma, this practice engendered my own belief that boys and girls should be friends.

Childhood confusion about religion

I thought Jesus Christ was the most exciting person I had ever heard about. Stories about him walking on water fascinated me. Oh, if only I could meet him and get some tips on how to do those things! Dad was always saying that anything was possible. So I imagined inviting Jesus to a neighborhood party where he could manifest an endless supply of Kool-Aid.

I did not, however, think it would be fun to play hide 'n' seek with Jesus. If he could go into and out of his body, he could sneak out of it and see where everybody was hiding. Nope. I'd just invite him to a party or go to a lake for some water-walking. The presence of Jesus Christ, Mary, and statues of saints made me think about being a saint. I thought performing miracles to help others would be the cat's meow. If those other humans could do those things, then I wanted to learn how to do them, too.

Mom was the only one in the family who read the Bible. We kids had Catechism to memorize and recite from. "Where is God?" "God is everywhere." At that time, however, the Catholic version of "everywhere" did not mean that we were a part of that everywhere.

When I was in grade school, Mom decided to become a Catholic so she could go to Church with us. She went through the study course with Monsignor Stimac, who was a wonderful, kind soul and always called Mom "Miss Sunshine." She really liked that. (And fortunately for me, I no longer thought *sunshine* meant the body's private parts.) Once Mom completed her studies, it was time to line up the baptism. Our family was so excited.

Monsignor Stimac sent papers to be signed by Archbishop Hunkler of the Kansas City diocese. Even though she had completed the requirements, the archbishop rejected Mom's request to be a Catholic. Because she had divorced RG, her first husband, the gates of the Catholic Church, and heaven, were closed to her. Monsignor Stimac told Mom, "I am so sorry, Miss Sunshine. You studied well and did a good job. I am so sorry."

Mom was flattened with discouragement, not to mention angry. She would remain condemned. In preparation for First Communion, which took place in second grade, each of her children learned that Mom was going to hell. Not only did the thought torment us, but each of us felt compelled to tell her this news. I can't imagine what that was like for her. And it was god-awful for us kids. I think we felt condemned too. One time I heard her mutter, "The Catholic Church and Hunkler can go to hell for all I care!"

We later found out that Jacqueline Kennedy's sister, Princess Lee Radziwill, was admitted into the Catholic Church after being divorced and remarried in circumstances similar to Mom's. However, Princess Lee had donated five thousand dollars to the Vatican.

This launched my questioning of religion and the Catholic Church. My mom was a good person, yet she was going to hell with murderers because she didn't have enough money to get baptized and saved.

All of us kids suffered great fear for our mother's soul. It was like being in a prison with no way out. We felt abandoned by the church, the same one we were required to attend every Sunday.

CHAPTER 4

Childhood Traumas

Threatened in the basement

Some childhood events were traumatizing but provided empowering lessons. I was nine when I was playing outside one summer evening. Dad was working just outside the basement door. I ran into the basement in the dusk light to get something, a toy. It was darker in the basement than outside, and objects were hard to distinguish, but I was in too big a hurry to turn on the light.

A dark figure a foot high was suddenly in front of me. It made a hissing noise and drew closer. I froze. A snake. Every part of me was frozen stiff with fear and I could not make my voice call for Dad. Still hissing, the snake jumped closer. I could barely hop back because of my stiffened body. Again the snake moved closer. I hopped back. This happened several times as the fear continued to choke my mobility. Finally, I managed to scream, "DADDDDDDDDDD!"

In an instant, Dad appeared. I was still frozen. He grabbed a hoe and struck the snake several times, making sure it could not move. Then he asked me if I was all right. He turned on the basement light and discovered it was a copperhead snake. He told me how lucky I was, that the snake was poisonous. I was beyond grateful that Dad showed up so fast and saved me.

That experience was the most demonstrative in my life thus far about how powerful fear could be. My own fear made me vulnerable to a near-fatal bite. I would never forget that. It was a turning point. I knew I had to find a way to win the war against fear.

A hole in my head

Later that same summer, a threatening ordeal created shock and fear in both Mom and me. One sunny day, Donny Mizell was in the backyard with me. We were by the thick bramble that led to the creek below. I bent down to pick something off the ground. I stood back up at the exact moment Donny was swinging a rusty shovel over my head to swat a bumble bee. The pointed rusty corner came down into the crown of my head, and a geyser of blood shot up. Donny froze.

"AHHHHHH! MOMMMMM!" I screamed and made my way toward the house. My fear at blood pouring down my face was more intense than the throbbing pain in my head. Then I stopped and stood in the driveway. If I got blood on the carpet, I would be in trouble. I kept screaming. Donny stood by me. Probably in shock himself, he said nothing. Finally, Ethel Stallard heard me. She ran out of her house with a towel in hand and called to Mom. After what seemed like an eternity of screaming, Mom appeared.

As she ran down to the driveway, I could see the fear in her eyes, and that triggered even greater fear in me. It is easy to go back and feel that moment in time. Her dark eyes always spoke the truth.

"Donny, go get your dad," Mom said as she began to help Ethel wipe blood from my face, my arms, my torso. Then, while Ethel stayed with me in the driveway, Mom called the doctor. Meanwhile Mr. Mizell, Donny's father, appeared. Dr. Speer told Mom to get me to town as fast as possible, instructing her to not let me sleep. He said to keep talking to me to keep me conscious. Because we only had the one car, which Dad took to work, Mr. Mizell agreed to drive us. I lay partly on Mom in the front seat while she kept a towel on my head. Fear ran thick in the atmosphere – mine, Mom's, and Mr. Mizell's. Mom kept asking me to repeat my name and answer questions. I remember just wanting to go to sleep, if only they would stop talking to me.

And then the unthinkable happened. Mr. Mizell's car ran out of gas on a country road. Mom's body stiffened like a pole. She gritted her teeth, looked down at me. There was a small house nearby. Rather strongly, she told Mr. Mizell to go over there and find out if they have any spare gas in a can. He rushed to the house and was able to secure a can of gas they had stored in their shed. Once again we were on our way. Mom's body relaxed a smidgeon as she continued to talk to me.

Mr. Mizell carried me into the doctor's office. Dr. Speer examined me, commenting, "Looks like Jannie has a hole in her head. I'm going to look around down in there, see what's going on." I cringed at the idea. At that time, an expression for people who did dumb things was, "They have a hole in the head." My child brain wondered if this would make me really dumb.

Dr. Speer determined the hole needed to be cleaned out. He cut some of my hair and proceeded to use peroxide and a Q-tip. As he dug around in my head, I felt like I was going to faint. When he finished, he sent us off with instructions for Mom on how to clean the wound.

I was a scrawny, puny kid, and prior to this, kids called me by the awful name "Uglystick." I already had low self-worth. Now, I was going to be "Uglystick" with a hole in my head. I thought it couldn't get much worse. It seemed my surroundings were pounding me into submission, demanding me to be less than I wanted to be. I was determined to survive, and wanted to come up with something that would give me some perks. I thought of dimples. Surely if I could make cute dimples in my cheeks, no one would remember that I had a hole in my head. For months I slept with marbles plastered to my cheeks. I even switched the type of marbles from steely pee-wees to larger shooters. Alas, nothing worked. No dimples. Not only was I discouraged, but the news had gotten out. The kids taunted me, chanting, "Jannie has a hole in her head!" What bothered me the most was hearing, "So that's what's wrong with you? A hole in your head!" I didn't think kids would *ever* forget about that. My siblings joined in. Ugh.

This is one of the experiences that has served my creative 3-D work with children. Fueled by a desire to help children know they can control how they feel, even when they cannot control their external circumstances, I developed fun, innovative ways to help preschoolers understand their inner resources by working with their mind, body, and emotions. I want them to know they always have a choice inside them.

A while back, my grandson was complaining about not getting to go someplace. He said he was sad and mad. I said it was okay to feel those things, but he needed to decide how long he wanted to feel them. He gave me a quizzical look. I told him to let me know when he was done feeling sad and mad, then we would do something really fun. I emphasized that it was important to have a good attitude. The longer he stayed mad and sad, the harder it would be to have fun. Not five seconds later, he told me he was finished with sad and mad, and he blew it out with a deep breath. We were able to have fun.

A decision too big for a little girl

I was ten years old when my Mom rushed me into the back bedroom and shut the door abruptly. I could see she was upset. She grabbed my shoulders like she would when she was angry. Then she bent close to my face, looked me in the eye, and in a strained voice demanded, "Jannie, tell me right now—should I get a divorce or stay married to your dad?"

My heart fell through the wall of my stomach. I felt sick. She repeated the question. It was clear she needed to know *right then.* My thoughts scrambled. The thought of not living with both of them frightened me.

"Tell me!" Mom insisted. "Tell me!" Finally, I said, "Stay married." She stood, let go of my shoulders, and said, "O.K." She opened the door to leave the room. I stood in total bewilderment.

I got my wish. Mom and Dad stayed married. What I didn't realize was that I would feel responsible whenever they fought. Countless times I thought: *It is my fault they are fighting because they are still married.* A sensation heavy with guilt strained my heart, then turned into sadness.

The heaviness of making such an important decision took its toll on me. The week following the big decision, Mom and Dad had a big blowout. Having no stress management skills or anyone to talk to, I stood and stared at nothing, and pulled out my eyelashes. Mom caught me and shouted, "Jannie, what in the hell are you doing?" It stunned me out of my daze. I explained that I wanted to count them to see how many I had. She looked at me like I was weird, and looked like she didn't know what to think or say. Shortly afterward, my eyelids became infected. We went to the doctor. I had to use medication while the eyelashes grew back in.

I wanted to lighten the fierce agitation that gnawed at their relationship. I worked hard to find lighted-hearted and funny things to share with them. How I longed to make them happy, but I had no idea that it was impossible for me to do. The stress was too great for a child. Later in life this experience would serve as a catalyst for me to help children find healthy ways of coping with stressful situations. Also, I never *ever* wanted my own children to deal with such a thing. Finally, I now know that no one can be responsible for anyone else's choice to be unhappy or happy. Lesson learned.

Playing house, and cowboys and injuns

A summer day that stands out as unforgettable was when my brother Ted and I were playing in the basement. We struck a deal. He would get in the baby carriage and be my baby, and I would play cowboys and injuns with him. We played house first. I had many errands to take him on. All too soon for me, he wanted out of the carriage. I begged him to stay a tad bit longer, promising I'd play his Wild West stuff longer, too. He agreed, but that didn't last long, and he got out of the carriage in a huff. "I don't like being a baby!"

It was time to play cowboys and injuns. Ted was a Cub Scout, so he could tie some pretty good knots. We went outside, and he tied my arms and torso to a post and said, "I'll be right back." Being tied up in the hot sun was miserable, and I wondered what he was up to.

Ted returned with his BB gun. I couldn't imagine why he brought it. He loaded it with gravel. Then he aimed at my legs and yelled, "I'm gonna make you dance, injun!" And that he did. From three feet away, he shot at me repeatedly, and I danced and screamed. I couldn't escape or protect myself.

I screamed and screamed for Mom. Where was she? Finally, after what seemed like three eternities, she came running outside. She grabbed the BB gun from Ted and hollered, "What is wrong with you? You are not supposed to shoot your sister! You are grounded from using this gun. And Dad will take care of you when he gets home!" We all knew that meant he would get punished with the thick leather belt. I wanted to feel glad he would be punished, but my legs were hurting. While Ted watched, gloating, Mom untied me and took me upstairs to attend to my injuries.

Ted got the belt when Dad arrived home. He was supposed to be grounded from the BB gun for two weeks. But several days later, they relented and it was back in his possession. I was mad about that and thought it was unfair. It was common for Mom and Dad not to follow through with the boys' punishments. We girls, on the other hand, always had to complete ours.

Did an angel help me save a life?

One evening, when I was ten and Karen was four, Dad had errands to do. He told us we could go for a ride. Our favorite thing to do on a summer evening was to go to the Lakeside Drive-In Movie dressed in our jammies and get an A&W baby root beer in a frosted mug, eat some popcorn, and watch a movie from the car. Oh how delicious that was! But on this particular night it was just an evening ride, probably to give Mom a kid-free evening. (Ted was not home that evening and Johnny wasn't born yet.)

In those days, cars did not have seatbelts. Karen rode standing up in the co-pilot seat next to the window. I sat in the back of the station wagon, the seat down and my legs sprawled out. It was dark and late. Dad liked to sing, and that night he was singing "Twilight Time."

Suddenly, I had one of those unusual experiences. In my mind, I heard a female voice say, "There is going to be a car accident. Tell Karen to come into the back of the car with you right away. Have her lie down next to you like this." Simultaneously, I saw a picture of what to do. The feeling of the experience was so serious that I *knew* I had to do it. I immediately called Karen to come in back with me. I took care of her often enough that she listened to me and climbed back. I told her to lie down exactly like I was shown. We lay there, me holding onto her, and not more than a minute later, our car was crashed into.

Apparently, two dragsters careened toward us from the opposite direction. The one in the far lane swerved toward the one in the lane closest to us, causing it to swerve directly in front of our car. It happened so fast that Dad had no time to put on the brakes. The crash was loud, intense. Dad's ribs were sore from hitting the steering wheel. His neck hurt from whiplash. But Karen and I were safe. If she had been in the front seat, she would have been thrown through the windshield. My mouth was cut up, and they couldn't tell how bad it was, so they sent me to the hospital. I felt so important riding in the ambulance.

Later, I tried to tell Dad and Mom about the voice and the picture. They didn't say anything. I was thinking that maybe I *was* crazy. I certainly didn't think I was holy, or good enough for angels to talk to me. So what in the world happened? Eventually, my thoughts just focused on the miracle that saved my sister's life. So many times I wondered where that voice came from and how it could see the future.

It created a knowing inside me that there is much more to life than what we see with our physical eyes.

Unexpected courage

I was baby-sitting Karen and her friend Debbie, who were both five years old. It was my eleventh summer. The day was humid, so I prepared a picnic for us to take on a fun outing in the woods. After finding a shady, cool spot under a tree near the creek, we had fun visiting and being silly. When we were finished eating, one of the Gerding Farm's horned bulls appeared. He dug in his hooves and flared his nostrils. No one was within yelling distance to help us. With two young ones in my care, I had to think fast.

I swooped Karen and Debbie behind a tree. "Stay right here. Don't move, no matter what!" They were scared, and whispered, "O.K." They knew by my voice it was a serious situation.

Keeping his eye on me, the bull drew closer.

"Stay behind the tree." I said again. The only thing that came to mind was what I had seen in the movies. I grabbed the tablecloth I'd brought for us to sit on—it happened to be red—and shouted, "Toro! Toro!" I moved away from where the girls were hiding. Then I realized the bull would come after the red cloth and me. The bull did a couple stomps with a front hoof. I was scared, but determined to protect the girls. I have no idea where I got the courage, but I decided not to waste another ounce of energy on fear, and started to wave the red cloth. I moved quickly, farther away from the girls, all the while shouting, "Toro! Toro!"

The bull followed me. His nostrils flared.

I knew I had to move even faster.

He stepped up his speed, too.

Running in zigzags to confuse him, I reached a grove where the trees were thicker. I ran behind a tree, wadded up the cloth, and threw it as hard as I could away from me. Then, holding my breath, I hid. I heard him go toward the red cloth and make breathy sounds. Moving ever so slowly, I peeked to see what was happening with the girls. Glancing behind me, I saw they were still hidden and quiet, a near-miracle for two little girls who both liked to talk.

Soon the bull moseyed away. I waited, and when I thought it was safe, I snuck back to the girls. In silence we quickly gathered our things and left. When we got far enough away, I let loose with a huge sigh of relief, and they followed suit. I complimented them for doing such a good job staying hidden and being quiet. Then the realization that I had just saved them from harm welled up inside me like nothing I had ever experienced.

Then another event grabbed our attention. Karen wasn't looking where she was going and stepped into a fresh cow pie. It stunk to high heaven. That was the day she chose to wear her new shoes. Well, that put a damper on what was our happy ending, but we were safe, and so very, very grateful.

Cow pies

Cow pies were a part of summer. When they were fresh and wet, we called them poo-puddles, and when we played in the pasture, we either had to jump over them or go around them. After a few days, the summer heat dried them up into pies.

One day, when I was eleven, I was playing baseball down in the pasture with the neighborhood boys. It was my turn at bat. That particular day, I was lucky and hit a homerun. I ran to home base and celebrated with happy shouting. Billy, the pitcher, had been striking others out, and he was *not* happy. Next to where I was celebrating was a big, warm, fresh, sticky cow pie. Billy picked up a large rock and threw it smack into the cow pie, splattering me. Dripping with cow pie, I was furious! Not only did it stink, but I was wearing my new outfit, pink shorts and a matching top, and now they were ruined. The stench overwhelmed my need to tell him off. I had to get home and clean up. Billy was the neighborhood bully. I often wonder why he was so unhappy.

Mom was furious about the ruined outfit. "I'm going to call Billy's parents. This is for the birds. He doesn't need to be so mean. He is a stinker. I'll fix his clock!" I think his parents apologized, and Billy was forbidden to go to the pasture when we were playing.

Clothes with color were special to me, a fresh contrast to the drab uniforms we had to wear at school. But money was tight all around, and the outfit was not replaced.

When I was made fun of, bullied, and demoralized during

childhood, I didn't know how to deal with it. I wished I knew how to make it stop. What I didn't know was that self-confidence and communication skills would have helped me. But we didn't think like that when I was growing up. Instead, most kids just fought bullies with punches, or they cried, or they tattled on them.

When I was bullied in the third grade about being puny and ugly, I told Mom about it. She told me to say something she had said to kids when she was growing up: "You think you're hot snot on a stick, but you're just cold boogers on a toothpick." I was surprised she told me I could say something like that. The next time kids made fun of me at school, I popped out with that little quote. It felt good, real good, until someone tattled on me and I had to stay in for the next recess.

When my grandson was three, he did an amazing thing with a bully. I took Jackson to a place for kids that had a pedaling-cycle that fueled a train running on tracks near the ceiling. (Very cool.) At first Jackson couldn't do it—too short in the leg department. But he was determined, and for several minutes he worked to make the train run. Finally, he scooted his buttsky up to the front end of the seat, held on for dear life to the arms of the chair, and managed to pedal strong enough to chug that train around the tracks. He was one proud preschooler.

Just as he was feeling the joy of success, a taller, older boy got up in his face and said, "I can make it go *faster.*" Jackson, still pedaling, quipped with equal pride, "I can make it go *slower.*" I was beside myself with proud Grandma Boom chuckles. How great to see such confidence in a three-year-old. He knew how to handle that bully. Then Jackson insisted Grandma Boom try pedaling to fuel the train. The device was too small for my body, so I was squished into a near-fetal cycling position. But I did it, and Jackson was thrilled. I was just grateful I didn't cramp.

Karen's awful ordeal

A neighbor girl known for causing trouble was riding her bike at the same time as my sister Karen was riding her hand-me-down bike with training wheels. Seven-year-old Karen rode along until the other girl viciously ran her off the road. Karen flew off the bike and landed on a rock, ripping apart her vaginal area. Mom and Dad rushed her to the hospital, where the trauma worsened for Karen. The nurses were abrupt and did not show the compassion to this little girl who was frightened, bleeding, and hurt. The doctor lacked bedside manner, and in fact, acted downright mean. Karen, frightened, ill-treated, and traumatized, kicked the doctor so hard that he flew back against a glass case, breaking some things. It is easy to imagine the flaring emotions in that room. It took several adults to hold Karen down. She must have felt like she was being tortured as they stitched her up.

When my parents arrived home with Karen, Mom handed her over to me. "Here, Jannie, you take care of Karen. Make sure she has whatever she needs. And don't leave her for long." Once again, I would be Karen's caretaker. Looking at poor Karen, I saw she was in such a deeply disturbed place, and her pain seemed severe. My heart filled with compassion for her. I wanted to do whatever I could to help her.

JFK's death

Our family loved the Kennedys, and I loved anything to do with them. I had even written to the First Family and received a personally signed photograph of Jackie, John, and Caroline. I was fourteen the day Dad and I were watching our Philco television. I even remember what I was wearing: pedal-pushers and a top with a mandarin collar.

President and Mrs. Kennedy were in Dallas, and the town was having a parade. Dignitaries rode in cars. The Kennedys were in a convertible. Then things got strange—JFK slumped over, Mrs. Kennedy held him, then she started climbing over the back of the car, men in suits started running, people were screaming. Dad jumped forward and clenched his fists around the arms of the chair. "What the hell? Jesus Christ!"

I sat stunned. My mind kept repeating: *It can't be true, it can't be true.* As people scattered in the streets of Dallas, the announcer's voice grew louder. My mind switched to other thoughts. *God wouldn't let this happen. Surely, the Catholic President of the United States had special protection from God. How could an all-knowing divinity let this happen?* At that moment, I believed God had made a mistake, which made him seem more human than divine. Mom's rejection by the Catholic Church already started me questioning my religion. JFK's death reinforced my doubts.

My mind and body were in shock, and I was afraid. If the protector of the country could be shot, that meant the rest of us were vulnerable. I wanted to grasp what was happening, and the best way to do that was to stay glued to the TV reports.

Mom came in, and when she saw and heard the news, said, "Oh my Lord! What in the hell is happening in our country?"

JFK's death brought our family together in discussion. We children had been left out of important discussions in the past, but that event affected us all so deeply that we couldn't help but share what we were thinking and feeling. It was the one time Mom and Dad actually listened to us in discussions, and our thoughts and opinions mattered.

Reflecting on the Kennedys brings up 9/11 and other incidents that have shaken our world. Regardless of age, everyone experiences the shockwave. I wonder what my grandchildren will have to go through. I wonder what they will need to be strong in the face of adversity.

Fallout shelters, the government, and Dad

Mom had her hands full when Dad was assigned a job with the General Services Administration to be in charge of the fallout shelters in seven states. She was working full-time as a receptionist at Procter and Gamble and caring for four children. We all had to pitch in and help with the functioning of the household.

Dad was gone a lot, frequently for a week or longer. For a number of years, he traveled more than he was at home. He had been in charge of the construction of the largest government building in Kansas City, Missouri, for GSA. He became aware of huge amounts of graft among some of the people involved in the project. He was furious because it was stealing from taxpayers. He reported the graft in the hope it would be stopped. He discovered that his report was not only unwanted, but those engaged in the graft decided to get him out of their hair. Knowing he had emphysema and difficulty breathing in cold climates, they started to send him to states with frigid winter temperatures, such as South Dakota. He was sure they were trying to worsen his health to force him to quit. He forged ahead in spite of the circumstances until his health declined so much that he could not continue. He began working on a lawsuit that was years in the making. He finally won the lawsuit, which satisfied him, but it could not return his health.

On his travels in that job, he learned many things. He knew a great deal about fallout shelters and their locations. He once confided in me that there was a huge underground city in the Denver area designed for important people to escape to in case of national emergency. He did not go into great detail, but said there were many secrets about that shelter, and that people like us would not be admitted into that haven of safety.

We had a basement for storage and protection from tornadoes. Dad talked about building a fallout shelter, but never accomplished it. School had students practice drills in case of fire or tornadoes—and for nuclear bombs. Part of the nuclear bomb drill was to hide under our desks. Dad told me that nuclear fallout could travel through solid objects and hiding under a desk would not help. He agreed with the practices for tornadoes and fires. However, he would always add that if we were out in the open with a tornado coming toward us to lie flat in a ditch. I can still see him holding up his pinky finger. "Do not even hold up your little finger. Stay completely flat in the ditch. A tornado could pick you up and swirl you into the sky if your finger was up and you were not completely flat."

Big Mama dies

The summer I was twelve, Big Mama became very ill, and Mom had to go to Florida for two weeks. Dad worked all day and went to Army Reserve meetings some evenings. That meant I would be in charge of my three younger siblings, including the baby, Johnny. Before she left, Mom gave me a crash course in cooking. I was nervous about the whole thing, but I really wanted to prove myself and be thought of as a capable young adult.

Although my hands were full, I was feeling my oats. Then one afternoon, the tornado siren blared. I yelled for Ted, who was supposed to stay within yelling distance, but he was nowhere to be found. I was beside myself. The winds picked up. I had to get the younger children to safety. Mildred Mizell called us to come over to their basement so we could be with an adult. So we went, without Ted. The tornado hit one mile from our house. It wasn't until the storm cleared that he showed up. He never would say where he had been. I was angry and felt like I had failed somehow.

Two weeks after Mom returned, Big Mama died, and we drove to Florida as a family. Mom was sad, and busy with details, so I looked after my siblings. This was my first experience with the death of someone in our family. Even though I was not close to Big Mama, I kept crying, which confused me. (I now understand that I was absorbing Mom's grief.) Mom gave me half a tranquilizer so I would not cry so much in church. It didn't help. I still cried, and all along wondered why.

Big Mama's death made me face the raw truth of our inevitable mortality. Before she died, I didn't think death could touch our family. Now I wondered how I would handle it if one of my parents or siblings died. I didn't want to think about it, but my mind was now open to the chances of it happening.

"Holding onto anger is like grasping a hot coal with the intent of throwing it at someone else. You are the one who gets burned."

~ BUDDHA

"It's a helluva start, being
able to recognize what
makes you happy."

~ LUCILLE BALL

CHAPTER 5

Weaving Fun into Everyday Struggles

Uncle Mark once told me I was a hedonist. I looked it up in *Webster* and surmised that he thought I liked to have fun too much. Playing and having fun, whether alone or with friends, were the highlights of my life. With all the stress at home and at school, I could go just so long without fun. Fun play was my built-in commercial break. I felt so good creating spaces and play where troubles were absent. Little did I know at the time that I was also creating endorphins, the body's natural pain-killers. I was using principles of self-help without knowing it.

We were not allowed to cuss like Mom and Dad, so we found sneaky ways to cheat on that, just a wee bit. We kids learned pig Latin. It was a juicy kind of pleasure to think we could cuss and fool our parents. We had no clue that they could figure out what we were saying. One day, after Ted had said something that included the word *ell-hay* (hell), Mom surprised us by saying, "Top-say ussing-cay" (Stop cussing). We were flattened with disappointment.

We still used pig Latin after that, but just for fun. We needed another way to talk in front of our parents when we didn't want them to understand. I don't remember how it came about, but the ONG language was born. It works like this: Add *ong* onto all the consonants and just say the vowels as they are. The word "friend" is said as: *fong-rong-i-e-nong-dong*. The word "love" would be: *long-o-vong-e*. We thought we were something else with our own language that our folks didn't understand.

One day I was trying cuss in ONG for the first time. Mom was in the kitchen. Karen, Ted, and I were in the dining room. I used a word Mom use a lot, "damn." In ONG language it is *dong-a-mong-nong*. From the kitchen Mom hollered, "Song-tong-o-pong tong-hong-a-tong, yong-o-u-nong-gong long-a-dong-y!" (In English, "Stop that young lady!") How long had she known what we were saying? We were devastated. It seemed impossible to fool our parents.

I still use pig Latin and ONG language today. I sing "Happy Birthday" to friends and relatives in both languages. And I can't wait to teach these to my grandchildren when they are a bit older. We *must* keep up tradition!

Playing jokes on each other and teasing was also fun, except when it got out of hand, of course, which, with four kids, happened frequently. And we loved to watch funny shows on TV, to be together and laugh, and forget our woes. It was the best.

One time, I had the giggles, which turned into laughter I could not control. Holding my tummy, I collapsed on the floor. Dad must have had a rough day at work or was upset with Mom, and he got angry with me. His voice, gruff with anger, burst through my hilarity. "Stop that laughing this minute!" I tried. I really did. Especially because he scared me. I took myself to the back bedroom, silent giggles still rolling out.

I Love Lucy was my favorite TV show. For a repressed girl with a dancing spirit that was caged, Lucy was nothing less than a savior. I gleaned hope from seeing a woman look pretty, wear stylish clothes, *and* have outrageous fun being silly. She got to open her mouth and make all kinds of sounds and comments. She was inspiring. I loved her.

Summer days

Summer days lent themselves to drinking Kool-Aid, getting wet with the hose, listening for the popsicle man, staying in the shade, playing indoors during thunderstorms, and playing dress-ups and games in the cool basement with neighbors. Going barefoot felt freeing. Sitting in the grass often meant getting chigger bites that itched longer than mosquito bites did. Evenings were sometimes hot and humid. Occasional visits to a public or private swimming pool were heavenly.

For many years we had no air conditioning. Fans were our saving grace. Mom kept a brown crock pitcher full of Southern sweet tea for meals and in-between. Kool-Aid was made up and kept in the refrigerator.

Classic Mom in the summer: short-shorts, cotton top, and flip-flops She looked good and dressed to show off her figure. She liked to tan, and we girls would join her on the aluminum lounge chairs. Mom liked to "chew the fat" with us girls while we all tanned. While she had laundry going in the basement, she took cigarette breaks out on the back porch. It was common to see her pick up the corner of her shirt and wipe the sweat that always seemed to be dripping off her nose. Regardless of the heat, she always had a good meal cooking on the stove.

Southern sayings were a part of her, as was cussing when she was angry. When school was out of session and we four kids were together for longer periods, sibling battles flared. Common expressions Mom used with us were quips like: "Don't be ugly!" "Pretty is as pretty does!" "Settle down. Y'all act like you've got ants in your pants!" "Don't sweat the small stuff." "Get off your high horse *raight* now!" "That's a piss-poor excuse!" "I think I'll mosey on over there." "Well… *hell's bells!*" "Shit, fire, and save the matches!"

When Mom was irritated with someone, sayings were more explicit. "He is so dumb he doesn't know his ass from a hole in the ground." "She's as nervous as a whore in church." "I feel like I've been screwed, glued, and tattooed!" "Dayum!" "Just kiss my ass smack dab in the middle where the sun don't shine." One summer when I experimented with red lipstick instead of the normal pink, I heard, "Take that red lipstick off. Your mouth looks like a hen's ass at raspberry pickin' time!" Pink wasn't so bad, anyway.

If her nose itched, she told us it meant unexpected company was coming or something was coming in the mail. Occasionally, we could get her to sit on the kitchen floor and play jacks. Boy, she was fast and good at that game! Some evenings she would play piano and sing, usually hymns. If something went awry with any of us kids, she jumped up from the piano bench and reminded us, "Li'l miss (or mister), you best walk a chalk line." If we complained or spoke up, she did not hesitate to tell us, "Don't you be sassing yo' mama if you know what's good for you." Occasionally, when someone farted, she would act like she was trying to catch it flying around the room. It was hilarious!

Classic Dad in the summer: Arrive home from work, change clothes, eat dinner, read the newspaper and watch TV. He was almost always smoking. He kept busy. Sometimes, he worked on a project in the basement or fixed the car, cussing when things didn't go right. He also freely gave lectures if he thought any of us needed one. On Saturday evening he always had a drink or two of either what he called a "Jan-hattan," named after himself, or a martini. Dad was proud of his skill at tossing popcorn, pills, and peanuts into his mouth with a quick snap of his wrist. He frequently demonstrated. I can still see him doing it. I never saw him miss. When he got older and suffered from cancer, he would launch several pills and vitamins in his mouth at the same time without missing. He said it was because he had an engineer's mind.

When Dad entered a room, everyone knew it. His presence permeated whatever was going on. In the summer, he delighted in giving us nickels for the Popsicle man. He enjoyed taking us to the outdoor drive-in movie at Lakeside. He liked providing us with experiences. I think he was in his element when he was being generous and providing.

Duct tape was his greatest aid. One special summer day, he called me to the basement, pulled down a duct-taped box, and opened it. Inside were the vases he had watched being unearthed in China, the ones the archaeologist gave him. He asked which one I liked the best and said some day it would be mine. I spoke up and said that Karen would want the other one. Agreed. Then he strapped the box closed with fresh duct-tape and put it back up on the basement rafter.

Cussing in the summer heat was not uncommon if something went awry in Dad's court. The phrase "son of a bitch" confused me. Sometimes he said this of women I knew, and I didn't think they were that kind of women, so why would he say that? When he was upset, his huffing and puffing and stomping filled the house. Mom called him as a "bull in a china cabinet." That never went over well with Dad.

Dad was the one who looked for bargains and kept the basement food supply stocked up "just in case" of storms. He also liked good deals, so we were never without extras of everything. It was another noticeable impact of his family running short of supplies during the Great Depression.

Summer evenings

Summer evenings were such fun. Lots of neighborhood kids would come out and play hide 'n' seek. We had tons of places to hide. We ran around among the flitting fireflies. These lightning bugs, as we called them, brought magic into summer evenings. Sometimes I longed to be a fairy with blinking lights just like them. One thing always gave me away when hiding, though. My digestion must have been off, because I belched a lot. Except these had a unique sound, and I called them "birches," meaning a half-belch/half-burp. When we played hide 'n' seek after dinner, I was beset with "birches," and they always got me caught. I enjoyed playing, anyway. I still enjoyed myself as I watched the game play out. I got caught up in the chases and shouted things like, "Hurry up! Run! He's right behind you!" Being a spectator could be as much fun as being a participant.

During the summers, friends came over more often. Mom and Dad had a special chemistry that people were attracted to. Most of the time, I preferred it if kids came to our house to play instead me going over to theirs. As a teenager, our home was a magnet for friends. Mom and Dad were warm and hospitable. In fact, when any of us kids had friends over, it meant Mom and Dad would not fight.

If Mom and Dad were in an intense arguing mode, and someone came to the front door, their arguing halted, and they put on a show like we were the Cleaver family on *Leave It to Beaver,* and everything was peachy-dandy. We kids were expected to switch gears, too. It was confusing, and I wished they could stop arguing like that when it was just us in the house. Still, I was grateful for my parents' strong personalities, which touched many people. Mom's Southern cooking made people drool, and more often than not in the summertime, we had company for dinner. Dad felt his home was his castle and it was meant to be shared. When we had company, Mom and Dad would bring out their best sides, be good listeners, and help out. More than once they extended their welcome to those having difficulties in their own homes.

Wintertime

Snowball fights and making snowmen, getting cold and coming inside for hot chocolate were highlights in the winter. The best thrill of all was sledding, especially at night when the moon was full. Our Jet Flyer sleds got work outs. Parents watched for cars while we kids sledded. We had so much fun, we didn't want to stop. Sometimes we went ice skating when the nearby pond was frozen over. Parents made a bonfire on the bank so we could roast marshmallows. Mom loved making fresh snow ice cream, vanilla and chocolate, when the snow was like powder. My memories of my childhood wintertimes spent outdoors feel so old-fashioned, quaint, dear.

Play and fantasy

Fantasy play was my favorite, from dress-ups, castles, and kings and queens, to detective work, western themes, and plays about being nuns and priests. I enjoyed making designs for costumes and imagining what they'd look like on me. There were many movie stars who inspired my fantasy play: Jane Fonda, for her raw courage; Elizabeth Taylor, for her beauty and jewels; Doris Day, for her radiance and for her singing that lit up generations; Lily Tomlin, for her sense of humor; Dolly Parton, for her wigs and talent; and Goldie Hawn, for her fun side.

We kids made up stories and new games, played baseball, skated, roamed the woods to look for arrowheads and crystal rocks, hula-hooped with friends, and so much more. When we played, we were free and happy. We created enlivening and colorful worlds that we wanted to live in. When I would play house, I would often hear the "voice" telling me: *You will have two children, a boy and a girl.*

Play and fun were the part of my childhood I wanted to take with me into adulthood. My inner child remains alive and healthy today because I keep her exercised. (Grandparenting is a wonderful stimulus for that.) For me, play is both a healing medicine and a preventive tool.

Family chores

To be a functioning family unit, everyone had to pitch in. Chores were divvied up. At an early age, I learned to dampen, starch, and iron clothes. Feeling capable of doing chores that helped out my parents helped me feel good. Karen was always helping out, too. The boys, more frequently than not, had to be reminded, nagged at, scolded, and punished repeatedly before they would finish their chores. Leniency towards the boys was an agitation for us girls. The boys still got the same allowances Karen and I did. We were all started at twenty-five cents a week, and we got raises in increments of a quarter.

When my own children were growing up, I kept up the tradition of family chores. By the time my children were eighteen months old, they knew how to fold small square washcloths. By age two, they progressed to hand towels and kitchen towels. I would start them out with singing, laughing, showing them it was fun while we worked together. Now, when the grandchildren come over, they help out by picking up toys. When I was a child, chores helped me feel needed. Even though they were a drag to do, especially when I could have been out playing, helping out made me feel better about myself. I wanted that feeling for my children and now for my grandchildren.

"Be someone who makes you happy."

~ ANONYMOUS

CHAPTER 6

Christmas Was Special and Difficult

On Christmas Eve we were allowed to stay up late. We would go to midnight Mass. The church was decorated, and a huge choir sang to celebrate Christ being born. I liked to think about him as a baby and wished I could have babysat for him. Before leaving for Mass, we got to open one Christmas gift. Mom loved watching us open gifts, and sometimes she hinted which packages we should open. Usually it was something like gloves, a sweater, or a scarf, things we could use for our special midnight outing to church. When we got home from Mass, we got to eat snacks.

And, of course, we woke up early the next morning in anticipation of what Santa Claus had brought us. The first sibling awake was supposed to wake up the others, then off we would go in our jammies, our morning hunger pushed aside by the thought of Santa's offerings. Mom loved Christmas morning. She liked to provide us with gifts and worked to stretch the money so she could. She was proud of what she managed. On the other hand, Dad was always a pill to deal with after we opened gifts. He would start out fine, but before the morning was over, he was in a bad mood. Then Dad and Mom would argue. It ruined the day for the whole family. It was tradition.

One Christmas morning stands out. Karen had learned how to decoupage and made something special for Dad. When he opened it, he tossed it aside and said, "What do I want with something like that?!" Karen was crushed. My heart sank for her. I wanted to save her from the pain, but it was too late; the damage was done. Some pains remain a long time. That one did.

The main gifts I remember Dad accepting from me were shirts I made after I learned to sew. He wore them proudly and didn't get mad at me for giving them to him. We all liked to give Mom gifts, and she was always grateful for anything we gave her.

Expressing gratitude for gifts from my own children when they were growing up, and now from my grandchildren, is such a joy. Their gifts bring the good memories of the past into the present moment to celebrate again. And, their artwork and mementos I keep in my home are living reminders that I am both Mom and Grandma Boom.

With all the contradictions the day brought, I still believe it is possible to have a truly *merry* Christmas. The conflicting Christmas experiences of my childhood planted a seed in me: My children would have fun on Christmas. I worked hard at it, and have been successful at choreographing many wonderful Christmas celebrations.

One of my favorite things about Christmas is the good will so many people express. As a kid, every holiday season I had a recurring daydream where I imagined myself as Santa and I went around and made everyone, including parents, happy. Most of all, I wished to turn a magical key that would happify Dad. (Yes, I make up words when *Webster* hasn't yet mustered up the right feeling with existing ones.) I never underestimate the power of happiness.

"There is no way to happiness.
Happiness is the way."

~ BUDDHA

"Thousands of candles can be lighted from a single candle, and the life of the candle will not be shortened. Happiness never decreases by being shared."

~ BUDDHA

CHAPTER 7

Summer Florida Vacations

Every summer, Mom longed to see Big Mama and her friends in Wildwood, Florida. Our visits were exciting: Southern food and hospitality, spitting watermelon seeds, playing at Daytona Beach, being with kids who had delightful accents, fishing with bamboo poles, eating sugarcane, and more.

Dad packed us up. His style, one that I have inherited, was to "pack just in case." Duffle bags, food to snack on, pillows, covers, and a little hand-held potty, primarily for me, were stuffed into the station wagon. Mom and Dad brewed coffee at home and filled their thermoses. The morning of departure, the coffee smell in the car was wonderful, like home on a peaceful morning.

Trips started out pretty well. We left at 4:00 a.m. and drove all day, all night, and the next day, straight through to Wildwood. Dad made only a few stops—for gas, to refill their coffee thermoses, and to eat at a restaurant. We were supposed to use the bathroom to "do our business" when we stopped. But I had to go so often, and Dad didn't want to stop every time, so they had a special hand-held potty. So while he sped at an average of 100 to 110, if I had to pee, I used the hand-held potty, then handed it up to Mom. Balancing carefully while Dad kept driving, she opened the front co-pilot door, held the potty low near the floorboard, and poured out the pee.

The high rate of speed, going around curves, and sometimes passing *on* curves (Dad insisted that he was an engineer so he knew how to pass on curves), upset me, and I learned to sleep during the long car trips. Driving straight through and being caffeined-up and weary, Mom and Dad never failed to get into arguments. That was another good reason to sleep.

As we neared Wildwood, excitement filled the car. Big Mama lived in a small white frame house with a front porch. The Cochrans' backyard adjoined Big Mama's at an angle. It was the Cochran kids—Sheilah, Teedlee, and Jimmy—that we were excited to see. After going through the niceties of greeting Big Mama and biding our time, we were allowed to go through the backyard and knock on the Cochrans' back door.

The Cochran kids were special to us, as close as cousins. We could play all the time and not tire of each other. Sheilah Cochran was my age and had the most beautiful black hair. I used to dream about what it would be like to have hair like that. Her dark eyes were captivating. And her complexion! She looked like a movie star to me. Teedlee was closer to Karen's age, and they were buddies. I loved Teedlee's life spark. She seemed more alive than most kids. She had a twinkle in her eye that meant she was going to do what she darned well wanted. She could put up a pretty good argument with her older siblings, and her sense of humor was priceless.

One summer, a skunk chased Teedlee and Karen in a garden, and they got sprayed. The intense, musky odor on them was unforgettable. The two of them had to stay outside and soak in tomato juice and vinegar for a long time. Afterward, they still smelled like skunk. Their clothes were thrown away. That year, we were staying at the Cochrans' house, and all the girls were sleeping in the same bedroom. The night of the skunk I had to hold my nose in order to get to sleep. Oh, how it stunk! This stuff never happened to us in Kansas.

Jimmy Cochran was full of it. One look at him and you knew why his mama called him Jimmy Dickens. That boy could tease the tail off a squirrel. He was always getting into things, and had the funniest way of expressing himself. When he had to go to the bathroom, he said, "Mama! My kidneys are a-threatenin'! My kidneys are a-threatenin'!"

The Cochran parents, Son and Annette, were close friends with my parents and like an aunt and uncle to us. We loved them and knew they loved us. The Mestroviches and Cochrans had an unexplainable bond.

Then there were Aunt Ethel and Uncle Henry, who were not actually relatives, but felt like it. I will never forget one time we arrived in Wildwood. It was hot and skin-sticky sultry. Ethel and Henry, bless their hearts, arrived with nothing short of a Disney fantasy for us: a whole homegrown watermelon for each of the "Mestroviches-from-Kansas." This was a first for us kids. The rest of the day broke out in spontaneous watermelon seed spitting contests. I still spit watermelon seeds, and I'm pretty good at it. A few years back, I won the watermelon seed spitting contest in central Oregon. I taught my technique to my kids, and now teach my grandkids. It's the kind of fun that catches everyone up in the present moment.

The Morrisons, Sarah and O.L., with their two spunky daughters, Vicky Dale and Becky, were regulars to visit when we went to Wildwood. Mom had gone to school with them. Becky and Vicky Dale played with Karen and me. Both girls were as cute as it gets. Vicky Dale was my age and tended to be bossy, so I learned how to be bossy back. Still, we got along well. Becky was strong willed and sometimes had a smart mouth. She also had this cute walk that declared nobody was ever going to push her around. She could get pretty ticked at Vicky Dale, and when she was mad, her lips stuck out, and so would her butt. She would raise her head and stomp off to make a point. I was amazed that these girls could mouth off and not get it trouble. Although I couldn't do that at home, it opened my eyes to the possibility that kids can be free to express themselves.

When I was little, I remember that black people in Wildwood were segregated from the white people. Not only were the black people not allowed to walk on the same side of the street as the whites, they couldn't go into the front door of stores and restaurants. I never saw that in Kansas, and I was struck with sadness to witness it.

Dad and Mom carried their prejudice all the while when I was growing up, although before she died, Mom opened up more. Even though I lived under the influence of prejudiced people, I could not hold that feeling. It didn't fit. My parents wanted me to think like them, to agree with their point of view, and I got in trouble going against them on this. All I saw was that human beings had different colors of skin. And, ironically, the whites were always tanning to get darker. None of it made sense.

One of the memorable activities near the Cochrans' house was when Teedlee, Sheilah, Karen, and I played "snake." We would take a black rubber hose of pretty good length and hide in the ditch after dark. When a car came by, we'd slowly pull the hose-snake across the road. Some folks speeded up and got out of there. Some wanted to run over the snake and kill it. They would stop and back up over it to make sure it was dead. It was such a blast. In our goofy way, we were tricking the adults. We laughed and laughed later as we retold stories about different cars.

I went on my first date in Wildwood. Mom had warned me if a boy tried to French kiss me it meant he wanted to go to bed with me. I was sixteen, and after we went to a movie, he drove me up to the Cochrans' house, where I was staying. Then that nice boy leaned over and tried to French kiss me. I heard Mom's voice inside my head, and all I could think to say was, "If you're hungry, why don't you go get a sandwich!" He didn't ask me out again. It was a clumsy situation. But I was glad that at least I spoke right up. That was not typical of me.

Every summer, we made weekend treks to Daytona Beach, heaven on earth. To ride the waves, we used canvas floats and inner tubes. I started at age three, and as of this writing, I have gone ocean-wave-riding for sixty-two consecutive years. I am "raight" proud of that record. Shovels and buckets were used for building sandcastles. I collected shells that dotted the sandy beach with their pretty little pearlized colors. It was another world.

In Daytona, Mom and Dad were not stressed with work and normal responsibilities, so they "chewed the fat" a lot. And when Mom and Dad argued, I stayed in the waves. The ocean cradled me with happiness. Nothing else existed. I rode the waves and let myself be lulled by their rhythmic, rolling songs. Catching a wave and letting it carry me to the shore was better than any circus ride. It was perfect play.

One of my most memorable experiences was when I was about eight. We were at Daytona Beach. Dad and I were in the ocean, Mom was on the beach tanning, Ted was digging in the sand near the car, Karen was by Mom. (This was before Johnny was born.) The weather changed quickly. Clouds rolled in. It became dark. Stinging rain pelted us. Thunder rolled around us, reverberating and shivering our bodies, which meant that lightning was close. Mom yelled at Dad and me to get ourselves out of that water "raight now!" Dad refused.

Oh boy, was I confused, but I stayed with Dad. Mom yelled, "Get out of that water RAIGHT now before you get killed from that lightnin'!" Dad loved to have the upper hand, and he loved to tease Mom. I looked from one to the other, waiting to see how this would play out. When I saw Mom's expression I thought if the lightning didn't get us first, she was going to kill us. But Dad chuckled and stayed in the water, playing with me in the waves. I finally got the gist of what he was doing. Whoa! I got a taste of the perks of power!

Then I glanced up and saw a brilliant streak of lightning. That would trigger Mom all the more. She was livid. I started to feel afraid. Then I remembered Dad was like God, so he must know we would be all right, and I started having fun again. For the first time, I felt like Dad and I were allies, and we were playing a wonderful game together.

Another, brighter lightning flash brought Dad to his senses, and he and I headed back. Mom's eyes looked like they were shooting darts as she watched us from the car, where she and Ted and Karen waited. Even from the shore, I could feel her anger. Dad and I ran to the car. Once inside, Mom lit into Dad. He usually fought back, but not that day. He just laughed, which perturbed her to no end. Having nothing to struggle against, she eventually let up. I kept my mouth shut and hid under a towel in the hope she would forget to yell at me. Even if she had, the joy of playing in the waves with my Dad during a storm was worth every ounce of getting in trouble.

Leaving Florida was hard. Especially having to leave the Cochrans. Our relationship with them taught me that we can also choose others to be our family.

From beyond the grave

It was 2001 and I was living in Oregon when I was awakened by the phone at 5:30 in the morning. "Hello," I said sleepily. No one responded, but I heard talking. I said hello a couple more times. It sounded like Sheilah and Teedlee. This was just after their mother's funeral. Teedlee still lived in Florida, and Sheilah lived in Oklahoma but was in Florida for the funeral.

"Sheilah? Teedlee?" I said, but they kept talking to each other and not me. It was beyond me why they didn't answer me. Maybe they didn't realize I had picked up the phone. I understood enough of their conversation to know they were talking about their mom and about goings-on at the house. I couldn't understand why they wanted me to hear this conversation anyway; it was private family stuff. So I hung up.

Later that day I called Teedlee and asked why they had called so early. Teedlee said they had not called. I repeated snips of conversation I had heard. Teedlee was astounded. She told me when they were talking about those things, they were walking outside. I told her the call registered on my phone as being from Sheilah, but Teedlee said Sheilah had left her cell phone back at the house.

This experience defies rational explanation. Sheilah thought it was their mom trying to make contact with them through me. Whatever the case, we all know something extraordinary happened. Some events don't fit our views of how the world works, and we just have to accept that they happen. Who knows, maybe Sheilah was right, and maybe we continue beyond the grave. These are the moments when I shake my head in bewilderment and I smile. My own unexplainable experiences motivate me to stay open-minded. Katherine Howe's quote fits here: "Just because you don't believe it is real does not mean it doesn't exist."

"The wound is the place where
the light enters you."

~ RUMI

"Let us always meet each
other with smiles, for the smile
is the beginning of love."

~ MOTHER THERESA

CHAPTER 8

Teen Years

Pre-Teen time and the training bra

As time passed and other girls my age started to develop, I became increasingly aware that I would never be their equal when it came to having a robust bust. Being the only girl who was not from a double-Croatian descent and having a small-boned mother, my chest looked like two split peas on an ironing board. My uniform hung on my body differently, and I wanted solutions. A budding girlfriend told me it would help if I put a hand on either side of the door frame and squeezed, and to do this every day. When I tried it, my arms were exhausted, but my chest remained flat. Being flat-chested just added to my already considerable feelings of insecurity. I hated that it was something I could not control. I had to fix this!

Even though I didn't need a bra, I talked Mom into getting me a training bra. My literal translation of the product's purpose was that it would train my chest to develop. When that didn't happen, I began to stuff the training bra with tissues. I found that if I slightly dampened them, they would wad together better to create more of the filled-out look I wanted.

Bra-stuffing was not without consequences. The worst was at the Wyandotte Swim Club. Some cute boys were there. I got into the pool and floated near them. Then, to my utter mortification, I saw one of my boobie-tissues floating in the water. I felt my face burn, and looked down. One side of my chest poked out and the other was flat. Quicker than Superman could have, I snatched up that tissue wad, hid it in my hand, and crossed my arms over my chest. I pretended to be cold and got out of the pool, and, walking as fast as I could without calling attention to myself, made a beeline for the bathroom. I restuffed my bra with fresh toilet paper, then called home for a ride. I did not return to the swim club that summer.

The vision

One afternoon, when I was thirteen, Ethel Stallard and Mom were visiting in the living room when my abdomen was stricken with pain. I was taught to not interrupt adults, but the pain was so intense I had to speak up. Mom and Ethel thought it might be appendicitis. Mom called the doctor, who told her to take me to the hospital to get checked out.

They took X-rays. It wasn't appendicitis, but they found a spot in my abdomen that puzzled the doctors. They wanted to keep me in the hospital overnight for observation.

When my parents left that evening and I was alone in the hospital room, I lay there, wondering and worrying about what was happening to my body. I cannot explain how, but suddenly, a light appeared in the room, and in my mind's eye I saw a vision of an ethereal globe slowly spinning. A voice in my head (I later learned this is called inner locution) said to help Earth. Children of all ages came to my heart. Then the vision and the light in the room slowly vanished.

This experience dazed me. I felt excited. My mind reeled with hundreds of thoughts. All my life I had wanted to know my purpose, and I saw this as confirmation that I was here to help. But the voice didn't give specifics. I surmised that joining the newly established Peace Corps was the only way I could get around to different places on the planet to help.

Oddly enough, the next morning the doctors took more X-rays. The spot they saw the day before was gone. They were bum-fuzzled. I was released to go home. In later years, I wondered if it had been important that I be away from the household when I received the vision, and whether the hospital was a neutral zone.

When I got home, I told Mom and Dad that I had had a vision and I was going to join the Peace Corps. Mom said she was now sure I was from Mars, and Dad said that I would *not* be joining the Peace Corps because I was finishing high school, then going on to college. I knew that authoritative voice, and that I would have no choice but to surrender to his mandate. Having the vision was both a blessing, for the guidance, and a curse, because I could not start right then.

My life needed a change

I was stifled in that parochial school, with their bland

uniforms and strict ways. After my sophomore year, I knew I could not bear to return. I had never spoken up to Dad before, but it was worth the risk to brave it. Gathering the courage was not easy. I designed a strategy: If fear struck me silent, I would kick myself, which would trigger me to talk.

I walked into the living room. Dad was reading the newspaper. I just stood there. Dad glanced at up at me, then back to the newspaper. My stomach knotted as my fear grew. I kicked myself. Hard. Dad must have been watching from the corner of his eye, because he looked at me with a quizzical expression. But the kick worked—I began to speak. My fear of having to continue to wear a uniform drove me to keep talking. He listened. He argued certain points. But I was so determined to switch schools that I stood my ground without being sassy. When I insisted it would be good for the family budget, Dad raised his eyebrows. Finally, seeing my arguments were sound and I would not back down, he succumbed.

This taught me a great lesson. As Dad really listened to how I felt, I saw how powerful it was to be heard and understood. I wanted that for my own children, and now my grandchildren. I wanted them to feel comfortable coming to me to discuss their feelings and ideas. The practice of listening wholeheartedly is integral to our development as confident and competent beings.

My junior year took me into a whole new world. I got to wear colorful clothes. I walked alone to school on a highway that was busy with traffic, so I carried mace for safety. I joined clubs, was in plays, and did volunteer work constructing homecoming floats. Students were easier to meet and befriend at Washington H.S. I did not hang out with one group exclusively, but made lots of friends in many different groups.

One day, my friend, Lynn, grabbed the mace out of my purse and sprayed it in class. Everyone in our vicinity started to cough and choke. The teacher came over and asked, "What is going—" and couldn't finish because he started coughing and choking. We ended up evacuating the room, laughing while choking. We could not go back into the classroom for the remainder of that hour. We wound up staying in the hall and having fun with our teacher. He was not mad and thought it was funny. I was surprised that we did not get in trouble. If this would have happened in a parochial setting, we may have been suspended. That was more excitement than I ever saw in school before. The adventure of it was wonderful.

American Field Service began during World War II with ambulance drivers. It developed into a cultural exchange program that allowed students to attend school in other countries. AFS student members organized events to help support a foreign exchange student who would attend our school. My senior year, I was secretary for the AFS and I was chosen to be the candidate for the AFS queen—and won. I never dreamed that I could attain an honor like AFS queen in high school. It was the first time I received confirmation from my peers that I was a likable person.

Raw adventuring in the Canadian wilderness

A friend, Ellen, excitedly told me about a canoeing trip she took during the summer of 1965. Leaving from Ely Lake, Minnesota, they had canoed and trekked into Canada. She wanted me to consider going the following summer of 1966, after my junior year, with other girlfriends— Janice, Susie, and Cheryl. We would be guided by the women who owned the tour company. Even though I had never camped or canoed, I begged my parents to let me go. One hundred and ten miles in seven days was the agenda. My parents finally agreed. I was both excited and fearful, and something awakened in me as I embraced the unknown.

We rode a bus to Ely, Minnesota, where we were trained for a day at the basecamp. We were not allowed to take any food. (However, I snuck into my backpack some of Mom's chocolate pound cake, which could withstand anything.) Our brief training included learning how to pick up a seventy-five-pound canoe and carry it, alone, over our heads. We also practiced carrying a sixty-five-pound pack on our backs. Portaging between lakes meant each person carried either a pack or a canoe alone. Part of our prep was to take loaves of Wonder Bread, place them on end, then sit on them. This smashed them to smithereens, making each slice paper-thin and the loaf of a size that could fit in the packs.

Following our three guides, the first day five of us girls headed out with bright eyes and anxious hearts. We had our first drinks from lake water and used leaves as cups. I felt like I was on expedition with Lewis and Clark. At one place, we stopped and slid down a short waterfall slide. The water was cold! I felt more alive than ever.

Having never pitched a tent, we all watched and listened to instructions from the guides the first night. We pitched one tent with poles solidly pounded into the ground. It felt stable for the five of us to sleep in. To keep from attracting bears, we tied the bags of food high in the trees. Then the guides informed us they had forgotten some critical supplies and needed to head back to basecamp. That meant we girls would be alone the first night. We were afraid, but fear soon gave way to exhaustion when we climbed into our sleeping bags and fell fast asleep.

During the night loud snuffling and grunts awakened us. Then the front tent pole on the tent just to my left fell. Frozen with fear, none of us spoke. Making as little sound as possible, I managed to tuck myself into a little ball deep inside the sleeping bag. We knew what was upon us—a bear looking for food. Hardly breathing, we stayed in position. I prayed like a soldier in a foxhole, while we listened to rumbling and ripping and snuffling. Then, it was silent. After a while, we crawled out of our sleeping bags and peaked at the collapsed tent. Fortunately, all of us girls were unharmed even though we were shaken from the bear scare. We saw that some of the supplies we had tied up in the tree had been pillaged. The bear got what he wanted.

When the guides returned, they were shocked to hear what had happened. After checking the supplies, they informed us we were a little short on food. They said it was too far to return to basecamp again. We could gather and eat berries and combine them with the dehydrated food we cooked over a campfire. We had fishing line and tried to catch fish, without success. We did have peanut butter, jelly, and that butt-smashed Wonder Bread. I was glad I had smuggled in Mom's pound cake, and every day I rationed a few bites for myself and my friends.

One day, we crossed a creek on foot. Balancing on the rounded log, and carrying a backpack that day, I did well, until my foot slipped. Down I went. I began to sink into silt. Sixty-five pounds of backpack pushed me down further. I was chest deep before the guides managed to yank off the half-submerged backpack, then pull me out. I was dripping with mud. I was not only grateful to be out and safe, but that there were no strange animals in there and I hadn't had to find out how deep that silt would have taken me. Fear was a frequent visitor on this excursion.

Another time, I stood in a shallow part of a lake and felt something strange. I pulled my foot out, and there were thirteen slimy, ugly, creatures stuck to me. Even between my toes. Leeches. They turned out to be plentiful on that trip. Often we had to peel them off. Pass the salt, please! It was the creepiest sensation.

We swam in gorgeous lakes, even drank from them, and no one got sick from it. At night, by the campfire, one of my friends, Susie, played the mouth harp. Her music was a perfect fit for the end of the day. There was no traffic there, no TVs or radios. Planes were not allowed to fly over the area. It was so quiet, so peaceful. The wilderness kissed my soul and I tasted the flavor of being a free spirit and one with nature. I was at home.

At the end of the 110 miles, a shock awaited us. We had left our belongings in the guides' locked cars. The young man who had helped us at basecamp before we left had stolen it all—our money, bus tickets home, extra sets of clean clothes ... *everything*. We were beside ourselves. How were we going to get home? And we had been looking forward to those fresh clothes. (Washing them in the lake did not get them nearly as clean as a washing machine and laundry detergent.) We felt violated, smelly, angry, confused, and let down.

We each had to do some quick problem solving. In the end, we all found help. I borrowed money from a guide to make a phone call to a friend's parents who vacationed in Minnesota during the summer. They were so gracious, came to camp, brought food, and loaned me money to wash my clothes and buy a bus ticket home.

The portage gave me a sense of who I was without others' expectations and limitations. I did not know I had such strength, stamina, courage, and prowess. An adventurous spirit awakened in me. I liked seeing more of who I was without restrictions on how I lived. For the first time, I began to like myself.

Continuing to discover more about my own potential and my own spirit strengthens me in aging. Being adaptable, flexible, spontaneous, and fun are all muscles of the spirit that continually call to be exercised. Being with young ones helps ensure that I exercise those muscles, as I encourage them to explore who they are through art activities and adventures.

From the wilderness to Washington, D.C., and New York

When I was a senior in high school, the teachers planned a class trip for us. We'd travel by bus to New York and Washington, D.C., to see the sights. I asked my parents for permission, and for the funding, since I didn't have enough in my savings. Mom was reluctant. Dad finally agreed.

Gettysburg, the Smithsonian Institute, Thomas Jefferson's home, George Washington's home, St. Peter's Cathedral, and many more places were on our itinerary. The cherry blossoms were in bloom, and the city spectacularly beautiful. At some of the sites, my body experienced ripples of sensation I did not understand. For example, Mt. Vernon felt familiar, and I felt at home there. Déjà vu played havoc with my mind as though I had been there before. Goosebumps ran over my body like a wildfire in dry grass.

While in New York City, we were given an afternoon to do whatever we wanted and maps to help us navigate. I wanted to go in a different direction than the others, so I took off by myself. I got lost. Geography has always been difficult for me.

I had never been in such a big city before, and somehow I wound up on skid row. I approached a couple of men who appeared to be living on the street and asked them to help me find my way back to the hotel. They smelled of alcohol and dirty clothes. Their eyes were sad. And they were extremely kind to me. They felt like adopted uncles. I know no strangers.

They studied the map and pointed out I had been following it backwards. Looking confident about how to get me back to where I needed to go, they said they would walk me back to my hotel. One of them was a bit...stagger-y, as we walked and talked. Before long, they had me back in front of the hotel. I was filled with gratitude and wished I could give them homemade cookies as a thank you. But I realized how genuinely happy they were to help, and to not be judged. For me, it was quite a lesson in power of acceptance.

When I went back inside the hotel, I discovered a group of students were organizing a search party to find me. It was a day of feeling cared for that I will never forget.

"Our own life has to be your message. You must love in a way that the person you love feels free."

~ THICH NHAT HAHN

"To be beautiful means to be yourself. You don't need to be accepted by others. You need to accept yourself."

~ THICH NHAT HAHN

Chapter 9

College Life at KSU

When I was about to graduate from high school, I was at my grandparents' house. Papa was outside, and Mama pulled me into her bedroom and told me, for a graduation gift, she wanted me to buy something I wanted. Her eyes lit up like Christmas as she handed me Kleenexes full of coins—quarters, dimes, and nickels, fifty dollars in all. How deeply touched I was! This meant that for a long time Mama had been hiding the change she had snuck from Papa. I appreciated not only the gift, but the joyful empowerment the "stealing" brought to her.

The day before I left for college, Mama shared some shocking news with me. We were walking down on the sidewalk in the late afternoon. She stopped, and in her broken English and with a troubled voice, told me that she hadn't told anyone this before, but she wanted to tell me what had happened to her in Croatia while she waited for Papa to send for her. With hand gestures and words, she told of being raped by soldiers. From the way she described it, I think it was a gang rape. At that time, a raped woman became an outcast and she carried that trauma her whole life. I was speechless. Now I understood why she always had such sadness in her eyes. I didn't want my Mama to have that horrible memory, that violation of her beautiful spirit. I wanted to say something that would take the pain away. We just stood in silence and leaned on each other.

A bit anxious about moving away from family, I left for Kansas State University. I changed curriculum five times in two years, trying to find a major that felt purposeful. Finally, Family and Child Development pulled my heartstrings, thanks to Dr. Betsy Bergen. She was an exceptional professor. In 1969, she was the first professor there to speak about homosexuality, stating that research had proven that there was a difference in brain chemistry between heterosexuals and homosexuals. She was an empowering role model.

My favorite class was judo, where there were only three females participating with forty males. Judo gave me strength. It also tuned me into the world of energy in terms of managing myself in challenging situations. I started to learn how to size up a situation, and then use it to survive and grow instead of letting the situation own me as a victim.

Sorority life began my sophomore year. The sorority nominated me to be in the Miss Kansas-Miss Missouri combined pageant. It was to be the first one televised live in Kansas City. Pageant time arrived, along with television cameras. Having been short-changed in the bosom department, I knew I would not make it to the pageant finals. However, the contestants chose Miss Hospitality. We each took our votes up to the judges. Contestants who didn't make the finals sat to the side of the stage. I took my shoes off and scooted them back under my chair. Then I heard my name. I won Miss Hospitality of Kansas. That meant the cameras were on me. Holy moly…I dug around under my chair for my shoes while the hosts quickly ad-libbed to get the cameras off me. Finally, my shoes on my feet, I made it onto the stage. What a moment! That experience went a long way to help me in my struggle with low self-esteem.

To earn money, I did office work with what was then called Kelly Girls. But the summer after my junior year at KSU brought an urge to do something to help children instead. I wanted experience in my field. A friend helped me land a job working six days a week in a state hospital in the children's cottages, where twelve severely disturbed children resided. They were given Thorazine and Mellaril twice daily. Each child lived in isolation behind a locked door. Some of them could come out for short periods of time if enough staff was available to manage their needs.

My heart was stretched in new ways. These children became my teachers and showed me what severity of abuse people inflicted on their children and what that abuse could do to the human psyche. I had never been exposed to such horrible life events as the ones these children had endured. I wanted to save them all. But being with them and helping in small ways was all that was possible. It became my priority to interact with them with play and fun. I longed to bring joy to these children who had none. And that summer, my passion for prevention was born.

They taught me that human potential can be nourished or it can be destroyed. I couldn't stand to see it squashed. Here are profiles of two of the children I worked with. (I have not used their real names.)

Valerie

As a baby, Valerie was labeled a "witch" because of the family's religious beliefs about a girl born with coal black hair and dark-as-night eyes. She had three older brothers and two parents who neglected and abused her in every way possible. At the age of eight she was removed from her home and put in a state hospital isolation unit for children twelve years and under.

Valerie never spoke. She was autistic and stared blankly. While the jury is out on all causes of autism, it is clear that if a child is born autistic, abuse can worsen the condition. Some theorists insist autism can be caused by severe abuse. She continually rocked, even when she walked. She could hear, but she appeared to have no feelings. No one ever heard what her voice sounded like. Sometimes I would just sit by her or read to her, tell her stories, and groom her silky beautiful hair. Three months passed. No response from her.

She was allowed outside her locked isolation room only when meds were distributed. I kept having images of being able to take her outdoors to water. After ages of pleading, writing requests to doctors, and meetings, I was granted the opportunity to get a toddler wading pool. It was a hot Kansas afternoon, and I was going to take her outside for a soak.

She had been locked inside for over two years. As we left the building, Valerie rocked vehemently, but she didn't refuse. When we got to the little pool, I sat on a wooden stool and put my feet in to soak. I told Valerie she could get into the pool and sit down. She stared at the pool, rocking back and forth for a moment, then entered of her own accord. Once she was in the water, she sat and rocked, causing ripples to go across the pool. She kept staring up at the tree that shaded us. After about half an hour, I heard a weak voice, "I wish I could eat worms." Valerie spoke! My wooden stool tilted and my butt landed on the ground.

I saw an extraordinary opportunity here. Lying with my half-cocked legs hanging over the edge of the wading pool, I said very quietly, "Valerie, why do worms sound good to eat to you?" Without looking away from the bird sitting on the branch in the shade tree, she replied with her heart's desire. "Because then I would be a bird and could fly away and be free."

My eyes filled with tears. All I could do was be with her in that moment. "I understand your feelings, Valerie. Thank you for sharing how you feel." She continued to stare at the bird. Two weeks later, I left for my senior year at college. I am told Valerie never spoke again. What an honor to be trusted with her innermost wish. Thank you, Valerie.

Bobby

A six-year-old boy who was the size of a two-year-old arrived at the cottage. He was the son of two people who lived in a shack. His parents were not fully brain developed. All Bobby knew to do was sit in a crib and eat hot dogs, buns, and chips. He did not know how to eat from a plate, or how to live outside a crib. He could not speak English, just made sounds that we could not discern. His muscles were so underdeveloped that he couldn't walk far without falling. His upper body, though, showed amazing strength when he hugged someone. He would unintentionally choke people with his hugs. Sometimes it took two adult workers to unlatch him from someone's neck. We wondered if perhaps he was hanging on for dear life, afraid he would be put back in the crib.

He couldn't relate to other children and was afraid of them. His eyes were beautiful but had a wild animal look. Bobby had to be worked with slowly as he learned how to eat, talk, walk, hug, and not harm others. The doctors' prognoses were that he'd never be normal. I wished I could have stayed to work with him.

These are just two of the children I considered my teachers that summer of 1970. It was hard to leave them, knowing their right to develop their potential was being incapacitated in that setting. But they became a part of the work I did later for children, and they live on in my heart.

"No one can make you feel inferior without your consent."

~ ELEANOR ROOSEVELT

CHAPTER 10

Peyote and Why I Don't Do Drugs

During my senior year I became interested in learning more about spirituality. That was shortly after I learned my siblings and I were part Native American. Mom hadn't told us before, because she had been ashamed of it. For some reason, she changed her opinion about having Native American blood in her DNA.

I had some good guy friends. We liked to spend time together as a group. On a gorgeous Kansas day, they invited me to join them on a trip to the country. I was game. We went to an abandoned schoolhouse with a huge field and a double-header (a two-person outhouse). The grasses were a foot tall and they swayed in the light breeze. It was a perfect day.

My friends said they were going to do some peyote and asked if I would like to try it. I said no, thanks, because I didn't know what it would do. I had heard Native Americans used it for spiritual experiences, and that part interested me, but my system had always been so sensitive that I was afraid to take one of the buttons. One friend suggested I take just a nibble. Craving spiritual expansion, I reconsidered and took a morsel.

It tasted bitter and was hard to chew. I wandered off into the grasses, feeling the beauty of the day. I lay down in the grass and felt cradled by the earth. And then it happened. I became part of the community of the grass and weeds. My consciousness moved into a space where I was communicating with them. I could *feel* their life force. I felt embraced. They were my brothers and sisters. Even though we looked different, we were connected. A vibrational frequency beyond any connection I had ever felt with anyone or anything settled into me. I did not feel alone. I was a part of everything around me, plugged in to the spirit of life. It was timeless. I had no compulsion or desire to move away from the experience. It was akin to the vision I had when I was four years old that showed me that we were all a dot and a part of God's "tummy."

At some point, my bladder called my attention. Slowly, my body arose from the earth blanket and I walked toward the double-header. I closed the door behind me and was so grateful I didn't go to school at a time when kids had to sit next to each other peeing and pooping. I remember thinking that having to raise my fingers to signify what I was going to do in the bathroom was better than having to share a double-header. My mind came back to peeing. I couldn't. It was strange—I felt the urge but I couldn't. I kept trying. Then I got scared, wondering if the peyote turned off my ability to pee. When would it come back? And what would happen if it took too long?

I cracked open the door and yelled to my guy friends to hurry, I needed them. They came right away and wanted to know what was wrong. I explained, and then told them I needed them to make sounds like water coming out of a faucet to induce my bladder to go. They laughed at first, then I straightened them out. They got serious and joined together to make water sounds. It worked! What relief…I thanked them profusely.

The peyote experience was powerful. I was grateful for what I saw and learned, and was able to integrate it into my philosophy and daily life. But I did not like losing control and not being able to pee. Thank goodness I had only a tish of the button. I decided never to do it again.

I was at Mom and Dad's when Mom asked me if I had some marijuana she could try. My sister and her friends were in the living room, and we went in there and all took a toke or two with Mom. She liked the details, which became more pronounced to her. Then she got up, saying she was hungry, and went to the kitchen to make brownies for everyone. I thought it was open-minded of her to try marijuana. Dad stuck with alcohol, and smoking until he got emphysema.

Over the years, I tried marijuana for migraines, and socially, but I enjoy just having fun in my normal state of mind. My sinuses prefer it, too. Natural ways to get high leave me feeling good all the way around.

"Our deepest fear is not that we are inadequate. Our deepest fear is that we are powerful beyond measure. It is our light, not our darkness that most frightens us. Your playing small does not serve the world. There is nothing enlightened about shrinking so that other people will not feel insecure around you. We are all meant to shine as children do. It is not just in some of us. It is in everyone and as we let our own light shine, we unconsciously give others permission to do the same. As we are liberated from our own fear, our presence automatically liberates others."

~ MARIANNE WILLIAMSON

CHAPTER 11

Family Deaths

Papa, my grandfather, was deteriorating. Finally, he couldn't be managed at home and had to go to a nursing home. It was 1968 and I was away at college, but I visited him on weekends. He would stare, unable to converse, just scream-moan like he was in dire pain. No one explained to us what was wrong. Perhaps they didn't know. I had never felt close to him, but I was grateful to him for all he had done to get himself and Mama to the US. When he died, he looked so much like he did in his living form—stiff. I was sad for him, for what he had missed out on in life. But I was glad he was not in such a difficult pain anymore.

The following year, Mama, my grandmother, got a flu shot. It took her down. She contracted the flu. I drove from KSU to the hospital in Kansas City to see her. Uncle Mark was sitting in the corner of the hospital room. Mama was in a coma. Speaking softly, Uncle Mark told me that Mama had not eaten or spoken for three days.

Uncle Mark frequently dabbed moisture on her lips to try to get her to take in some water. I lovingly moistened her lips while I was there with a wet cloth dipped in water. I spoke to her, no response. I touched her hand, which I had always loved to hold, and just stood there, being with her. Uncle Mark and I talked a little, but mostly I just stood there, knowing it was the last time I would see her alive.

Finally, I had to leave, because I was in the middle of tests at school. It was hard to turn toward the door. My feet felt like cement blocks. Uncle Mark saw my struggle, and he came over and handed me spending money. He was always so kind like that. I tried to refuse, but he had the last word. I turned back to Mama again and stood there as Uncle Mark returned to his chair. Then I told Uncle Mark, "I better go now."

In a light voice, Mama spoke, "Don't go. Don't go. Don't go." I gasped. Uncle Mark jumped up from his chair and came over to the bed. Mama's eyes remained closed. "But she has not said anything in three days!" he said. We were sharing a miracle, and looked at each other and connected in a way that we had never done before. But Mama was still not moving. We didn't understand.

After the shock wore off, and with great hesitation and deep sadness, I left. Yet something inside me was so grateful to know how much I meant to her. Uncle Mark later told me that those words Mama spoke to me were her last ones.

When she died, Dad was in the room. Once he shared with me that he saw Mama's spirit leave her body when she took her last breath. It was special that he witnessed it, but even more amazing that he talked about it.

When she finally let go of life, I was back at KSU. After I got the call, I cried and cried—my Mama was gone. At the viewing of the casket, I bent to kiss her goodbye. Her lips were so cold, waxy, stiff! What a shock. A light turned on in my mind: Her energy or spirit was not in her body; her flesh could not be warm anymore. It was a strange and eerie experience that opened my eyes. Still, I could feel her presence in the room. I felt her next to me, and knew her warmth.

Many months later at midnight Mass the following Christmas, I was back at St. John the Baptist Church with Dad and my siblings. During Mass when the singing was at a lull, I felt Mama next to me in the church pew. How I wanted to see her in her babushka and simple print dress…. I heard her voice in my head. She wanted to give me something. "Honey, my gift to you is all the compassion I gained in my life. It is now yours." Swoooooooosh. Something entered my heart area. I almost fell back in the pew. It felt as if I were being physically injected with a lifetime of compassion. I could not comprehend this with my mind, but I felt it in my body. Finally, I communicated with my mind and heart to her: "I don't understand, Mama, but I feel it. Thank you. I love you so much and I miss you." Then she was gone.

In 1970, Aunt Kay, my dad's sister who had lived with her parents throughout her adult years, died. I visited her at the hospital. We were informed she was terminal, diagnosed with cirrhosis of the liver due to alcohol consumption. How sad. She never had friends, had lived with her parents all her life, lost her boyfriend in the war, worked and came home every day, and drank to keep herself going. Such a lonely soul.

The following year, Uncle Mark died. He never told any of us that he had heart trouble. A bit overweight, he had been on heart medication for years. We never knew, and I didn't want to believe he was gone.

I helped clean out his room. All I could do was sit in his bedroom for a while, like I was visiting with him. Then an unexplainable experience occurred. I could smell the cherry tobacco that he loved. I didn't see the smoke, but I felt his energy. I spoke out loud, told him how important he had been to me and how much I missed him. I wanted to reach across the veil between life and death and give him a hug.

A few months later, another extraordinary experience occurred. One evening, a strong sensation was present in my room. I saw some spirit lights. They were beautiful colors, some small as pennies, others as large as fifty-cent pieces. They were blinking around the room in their otherworldly colors. Blue-white and a cross between purple, blue, and fuchsia were the main colors. I could feel the power of the incoming energy. Then with my physical ears, not inner locution, I heard Uncle Mark's voice. It sounded strained, like he was using all his might to say my name. "Jannie." He strained and said it three times. I was so shocked that I thought I was going to faint. All I could do was say his name back. "Uncle Mark. Uncle Mark." The energy stayed in the room for a while. I sat with it, feeling love for my uncle.

My mind was reeling with so many thoughts. How and why was it possible for me to hear his actual physical voice?

Most of all, what was he trying to tell me? My answer came two months later.

I learned that Uncle Mark had left me as the beneficiary of his estate to divide everything up for us four kids. He left his love and one dollar to Dad, his younger brother. Dad was furious, and told me to go back to Manhattan, Kansas, and wait to deal with the estate at a later time. I didn't think anything of it. I was taking a class on death that also covered the topic of wills. In my class, I learned that if the beneficiary does not execute the instruction in the will within nine months of the death, then everything goes to the next of kin. The nine-month mark had just passed, and I am sure Uncle Mark had been trying to tell me that when he called out my name. Dad received the house and financial assets.

I felt horrible for disappointing Uncle Mark and not carrying out his wishes. I hoped he could forgive my ignorance. And I felt betrayed by Dad and lost trust in him. To heal myself, I had to accept that he felt as next of kin he had more right to the money than his children did. I forgave him in my heart. The most important thing was that Uncle Mark honored all of us children enough to want to give his assets to us. That meant the world to me.

"The weak can never forgive.
Forgiveness is the attribute
of the strong."

~ MAHATMA GANDHI

CHAPTER 12

First Marriage and Why I Don't Drink Alcohol

Just before graduating with my B.S. in Family and Child Development, I got married. It lasted two and a half years. During that time, we traveled to Mexico for three months on three hundred and fifty dollars. Gas was cheap, and we camped on uninhabited beaches and cooked over campfires.

One night, two young Mexican men approached us when we were camping alongside some other Americans. They offered us homemade tequila. I never really liked alcohol. I rarely drank, and then only with friends. Just to get it down, I would mix beer with Coca Cola. That night in Mexico, we had some fruit juice and mixed the tequila with it. I decided to try it. The juice must have camouflaged the intensity of the alcohol content. I got drunk. I vaguely remember climbing on top of our car. There was a full moon that night and I decided to make it a double full moon with my bare butt after jumping on the roof of my car. How embarrassing! The worst part of it was we didn't have bathroom facilities, and all night long I had diarrhea and was vomiting at the same time in the bush. It was the most miserable night of my life. The next day I was completely wrung out. Others reported to me, though, that my antics had been quite funny. I made a decision. I like to have fun at a party, *and* I really like feeling good the next day. I never wanted to get drunk again. Losing control was not a way I wanted to party or live.

On that trip, I learned that my husband did not want children. In addition, my spiritual and intuitive side collided with his philosophy. I knew it was over. That July, I separated from him, and we divorced.

Before we left Mexico, we were camping at the edge of a bay, and we met an American woman who lived there. She befriended us and told us there were scorpions near our campsite, and invited us to move closer to her house. Then she invited us to a cookout. A young fisherman named Alfego was also invited. After dinner, Alfego offered to do a Tarot card reading. I didn't know what that was, but I was game. He told me many things that were accurate, including information about my upcoming divorce, which was not known to anyone. Alfego also indicated my work would not take off significantly until after I was sixty years old.

CHAPTER 13

Back to School at KSU

I was hungry to learn things that would help me with my vision to help the planet. I returned to Manhattan, Kansas. As a single divorcée with sixty dollars in my pocket, I wanted to get a M.S. in Family and Child Development. First, I had to earn some money. Waitressing eleven hours a day, six days a week, gave me bloody heels and some financial support. I lived in a communal situation where I had my own room and cheap rent. I was initiated into the practice of Transcendental Meditation. It allowed me to explore my inner world. I also heard about a technique called guided imagery. I was fortunate to have Dr. Stuart Twemlow mentor me with imagery and visualization, relaxation techniques, and transpersonal psychology. I was also intrigued by induced states of consciousness, which were also within his area of expertise.

I volunteered at a halfway house for criminals, and began to apply what I was learning. They had not been exposed to this alternative, self-help lifestyle, and loved what I was teaching them.

I received an assistantship in the Master's Degree program. On the recommendation from Dr. Tony Jurich, with whom I had the assistantship, I applied to be a co-director of Teen Outreach in the inner city area of Manhattan. This program for troubled youth was sponsored by a church, which provided basement space for the center.

I was warned by the board of directors that the youth were quite proud of their record: No one hired to work with them had stayed more than two weeks. When they hired me, I made a commitment to work evenings and that I would stay for one year. They looked at me like, "Sure you will."

The youth started testing me the first evening of duty when, as I left on my bicycle, some of them threw glass Coke bottles, which hit the wheels. The second night, they tried calling me names and they threw supplies. I announced to them that I was staying for one year. They laughed.

Close to the two-week record mark, they tried something new. I was going to the bathroom, which had a double-lock door. While I was peeing, the door burst open with a huge bang. Several teens had used all their body power to blast the door open. They caught me with my pants down, midstream. I grabbed my pants and pulled them up as fast as I could. They laughed. Their faces said they were certain I would leave. They went out to the alley. I couldn't wait to face them. In the alley, I scanned their faces, gave them direct eye contact, and slowly said, "I... am...staying...for... one...year." Their faces deflated like punctured balloons.

Testing and bullying continued nightly until a grave situation arose. Halfway through the evening, someone asked for the Ping-Pong supplies. At the bottom of the stairs that led to the alley was an activity supplies closet. Its door was locked with a flat lock. On my jeans hung a huge metal loop with a ton of keys, so it took a while to find the right key. Then I had to tip-toe to get the key on my jeans loop high enough to unlock the door. When I got the key in the door with my right hand, I had to place my left hand on the door to pull it open. Just as I inserted my left hand, middle finger, into the crevice to pull the door open, it was kick-slammed shut on my finger by someone behind me. My finger was jammed in the door, and the door was still locked. I smelled alcohol and felt the warm breath of someone breathing down my neck. Danger filled the air. My nervous system began blaring alarms. The only way to unlock the door was to again find the key on the metal loop with all the other keys. Somehow I did, and on tiptoe, I inserted the key into the flat lock, turned it, and pulled the door open. I looked at my left hand. The middle finger from the top knuckle up to the fingertip was split open to look like a book, a bleeding book. I turned around to find Ry, sixteen years old, one hundred eighty pounds, and drunk, hovering over me. In an instinctual act of survival, I looked him straight in the eye and threw a powerful punch to his jaw with my right fist. Ry's eyes widened. So did mine. It was as though the punch woke him up. He turned and walked up the stairs, and walked out.

After he left, I ran up the stairs and found someone to take me to the hospital. It took five stitches to sew my finger book back together. Then I went straight back to Teen Outreach.

Several teens were gathered in the alley, and they were quite surprised to see me. I stood in front of them, scanned the crowd to catch everyone's eye. They were silent. In a firm but friendly voice, I said: "I AM STAYING FOR ONE YEAR." I will never forget their looks of glazed shock.

After that, the criminals at the halfway house began to escort me to work and back each evening. The real criminals were a threat to the teen wannabe criminals. No one dared do anything to me.

Three weeks later, Ry showed up. He asked to speak with me privately. He thanked me for slugging him. "I don't want to tell you what I was going to do to you that night. Your slugging me in the face stopped me. Thanks." My knees were wobbly. I didn't want to imagine what would have happened if my survival instinct hadn't kicked in. Ry wound up sharing why he was upset that night, told me about his troubled mother and many other issues that confronted him.

After that, the other teens began confiding in me. It is what they needed. They shared their hearts, their lives, and taught me so much about potential. I am grateful. And I stayed for one year. I had to leave to tend to my school responsibilities, but they didn't want me to go. They live in my heart.

CHAPTER 14

Opening Up

As I worked on my master's, I was opening up on all levels. I began to develop my own views about child development, families, and what was possible. I was fascinated by emotionality and its role in intelligence, healing, self-sabotage, and more. Spiritually, I explored many new techniques and ways to see beyond physical reality. Finding new ways to exercise the body, such as yoga, also presented new experiences of body awareness.

In a workshop, I asked a Tibetan monk what the role of our emotions was. He paused, looked me deeply in the eyes. He seemed to be looking into my soul. "Emotions are a feedback system to let us know where we are in our evolution." Whoa! Pow! That set in motion a whole new avenue of exploration for me: epigenetics, going beyond genetics and environmental conditioning. I wanted to know how to do this in order to create a fuller, happier, healthier life.

Another landmark experience opened me to new horizons. On the K-State campus, I was in a meeting with the head of the Family and Child Development Department, three graduate students, and two professors. Sitting across from me was a student I barely knew. As we were discussing some theories, I saw the young man's face change, morph into different faces. It was like being in a sci-fi movie. At first I thought my eyes were having difficulty. I continued to stare. As I watched, his face change three times and look like three different people, I heard a voice inside my head informing me who each person was in a past life. I was told where each person got stuck with life lessons and how this had influenced the man's unresolved issues today. The voice stopped talking, his face stopped changing, and I knew why this person was unhappy, what he needed to do, and how.

I hadn't even heard of the concept of reincarnation and past lives. Now I tried to grasp the information, the *knowing*, that the energy inside us doesn't die with the body. I knew seeing this was a gift, and I had a responsibility to use it wisely.

I approached the student whose past lives I saw. In discussion, I learned that he believed in reincarnation. I shared my experience with him. I told him what I saw, the dynamics I was "seeing," and where it looked like he was blocked. He confirmed that the issues I reported were the ones he was dealing with.

Why was this happening? Why was I able to see it?

I found my gift to be invaluable in creative therapeutic work. It cut to the quick and helped me to help others. I rarely bring up the topic of past lives, because most of those I work with do not believe in reincarnation.

When I began practicing biofeedback, my awareness and

choices expanded. I loved being able to work with the resources inside me, understanding that every change in my thoughts had an impact on both my body and my emotions. I had never realized how connected they were. Typically, my colds lasted two weeks, but when I relaxed and focused warmth over my sinuses that I measured with a biofeedback instrument, my cold dissipated in three days. I was accessing more of my human potential.

I began working with young children, teens, the mentally disadvantaged, and families with great success, and kept track of what was working. I used visual aids to teach others about the world inside them. I developed a 3-D approach, which I have now used for four decades. It was birthed to accelerate self-help. It was exhilarating to teach others, many of whom had never realized that the mind, body, and emotions work together, how to access their own internal resources. By now, I knew that human potential included much more than just cognitive development.

As time passed, more things happened that continued to open me to expanded horizons in human potential. Dead people started contacting me right after their transition if I knew them or their relatives. Even if I couldn't see a physical form, their presence was undeniable. In most cases, they wanted to relay information that would help loved ones still alive. In some ways, my life was becoming more than I thought it would be. Although it did not bring many financial rewards, my work with children remained a steady force in my volition; my passion, the vision I carried in my heart and soul, was being fueled.

One of my professors, Dr. Ken Kennedy, was knowledgeable in the field of metaphysics, and he, along with Dr. Twemlow, guided me and helped me to understand some of what was happening to my awareness. They thought me fortunate to be so aware and alive. But there was just so much I did not understand.

CHAPTER 15

The Wonderful World of Momhood

Finally, my babies!

I married again, and immediately, an unfamiliar phenomenon began to occur. A beautiful, blue-white spirit light began to blink around me. It was the size of a silver dollar. I asked what its purpose was, and an inner locution voice said it was a spirit that wanted to be my child. Hungry to have my babies, I agreed. Soon, I conceived. It was such a beautiful spirit light. I felt honored. And becoming a mom was a lifetime dream come true.

During my first pregnancy, I intended to have a home birth, so I walked two to three miles a day (as I did later during my second pregnancy), both for my own strength as well as because I knew the motion rocked my baby. During labor, twenty-four hours came and went, and I knew I had to go to the hospital. My sister, Karen, helped with this process and was an invaluable support. As it turned out, a C-section was necessary.

Just before they put me under with general anesthesia, my baby's spirit light, so large now, appeared above my abdomen where they would make the incision. I heard a voice speak to me through inner locution: *Everything is going to be okay.* I was happy.

When they brought my daughter to me, she was crying in the nurse's arms. The second she was placed in my arms, she stopped and started to coo. She knew I was her mom. It was the most momentous moment of my life thus far. I wanted to keep her in the room with me, instead of them bringing her back to the nursery, which was policy at the time. I fought fiercely, and won. I sang John Denver's "Annie's Song" to her countless times.

As I grew accustomed to the mom-reality, I knew I would have another child down the road, and that I did not want general anesthesia again. After the C-section of the first birth, the aftermath of the general anesthesia was horrid. I coughed up green balls, felt emotionally distorted, had strange body sensations, and recovery was a prolonged affair. I never wanted to repeat the experience. So, I began to explore what I could do for the second birth, which still felt years away. Between now and then, I had to learn more about pain control and what the mind and body could do.

My first practice with pain control was to have a root canal with no pain meds before, during, or afterwards. First, I used my will: *I AM going to do this.* Second, I figured out which skills would support me in doing this: deep, slow breathing, having a calm center, and using imagery. I did not focus on "ouch," because I knew it causes more tension.

Will and skill did it. The feeling of success would prove to be nothing short of ecstatic.

Five years and more root canals later, I was ready to birth my second child. My ob-gyn was very open-minded and progressive. She understood what I wanted to do if vaginal birth was impossible and a C-section was needed. She gave her blessing for me to attempt delivery without anesthesia. Unfortunately, she was on vacation when I went into labor. Dr. Pheutse, the oldest practicing surgeon in Kansas at the time, was on duty.

I went into labor the same day I finished writing a book on assertiveness training. My husband at the time had decided to attend an out-of-state conference. Once again, my sister was an invaluable support, and when I went into labor, Karen took me to the hospital, an hour away. "False labor. Come back when the pains are closer together." False labor my ass! There was nothing false about the pain I was coping with. Karen drove us back home. Four days into labor, the father of my child returned home. Labor came on stronger at that point.

When I explained my wishes to Dr. Pheutse, he raised his eyebrows. I explained what I had done with root canals. His looked incredulous. "My son is a dentist," he said. "I know it is no small feat to have root canals without pain medication. Normally during a C-section, I inject 55 cc's of my pain concoction into the abdomen. As the surgery progresses, I add more as needed. I want to give you a chance to deliver as you wish. But for my own peace of mind, what I will do is compromise with you. I will give you only 10 cc's, and the anesthesiologist will stand by if we need him. That is the best I can offer."

My second favor was to ask to play music in the surgery room. Patients requesting music during surgery was unheard of in 1981 in Kansas. Dr. Pheutse granted my wish, and that morning Canon's version of "Seraphim Pachelbel" filled the sterile white room. The music attuned the medical personnel to a happy state. They commented how wonderful it sounded. Sun shone through the high windows, giving the room a soft glow.

They strapped my arms and legs down, and the surgery began. The 10 cc's injected in me did nothing. I could feel every sensation. For the first time, I was aware of all the cells in my body vibrating. I felt so alive. I was aware of the pain, which may have been considered excruciating if I chose to translate it that way. Instead, my focus was on deep breathing and using imagery to keep calm. The medical staff spoke in quiet tones, and the music and the soft glow of the sun shining through the high windows added a quality of softness.

During the procedure the anesthesiologist kept asking me if I needed medication. No, I told him, I was fine using my breathing and imagery. The incision that was cut to pull Darion out was too small. They used forceps. It felt like all my guts were being sucked out of me, but it was Darion. While one of the nurses loosened the straps on my arms and hands, Dr. Pheutse held my little boy up. I partially sat up, looked into his eyes, and said, "I love you."

Lying back again, the nurse re-strapped me and asked if I needed anything. "Nothing. I am happy." After I was sewn up, I requested a drip of Vitamin C and B-complex instead of glucose. They accommodated me. The endorphins produced by the pituitary gland and nervous system from this extraordinary experience kept me high for days. The pain was present, but it did not own me. I owned the day and gave birth my way. I was elated knowing that human potential had been given an opportunity to be expressed. Another great benefit of having had the baby this way was that I healed faster.

When they brought my baby, I was in heaven. Dr. Pheutse came to see me later. With graying hair and eyes that had seen many things in his day, he looked at me and said, "It's an honor to work with someone who is so intelligent. Thank you for what you just did. It is a high point in my work." Then he shook my hand. At that moment, my value of myself changed. No one had ever told me I was intelligent. It was a new experience that helped me with my self-worth.

I was determined to create the best life possible for my children, to give them what I didn't have, and to relay the good things I had learned from my past. I loved being a mom.

"Life isn't about finding yourself. Life is about creating yourself."

~ GEORGE BERNARD SHAW

Chapter 16

TV Work

Between my first and second pregnancies, I received a vision when I was meditating. I saw a beautiful, clear crystal. It was inside me. I saw myself doing television work, and the inner voice said I was to be like a crystal, radiating rainbows into the minds and hearts of children through television. How was I going to do that? No budget. No training. I had no idea what this meant, but the vision kept recurring. Then I discovered we had a local cable TV network that allowed community members to use the equipment free of charge, and I jumped in. I invested four hundred hours without pay. There were so many things I wanted to help children learn about themselves. For visual aids and 3-D symbols, I gathered things from around the house such as toilet paper holders and children's toys, I put together twelve half-hour programs that aired in Manhattan, Kansas, and later in Kansas City. By popular demand, the series aired two more times in Manhattan. I had a television pilot on my hands.

As serendipity would have it, an investor learned about my series. As executive producer, he made connections with

NBC in Wichita, and a deal was struck. Based on my pilot series, *Let's Look Inside,* a new children's series entitled *One of a Kind* emerged. I was the Rainbow Lady, and co-producer, creator, host, lyricist, and scriptwriter, as well as helping to direct and choreograph. Just after the series was produced but before it aired, I was flown around the Midwest to do promotional work. I was pregnant with my second baby. He caught the video bug that he enjoys in his life now. The series aired in four states.

Later the series won second place, silver medal, at the NY Film and Television Festival. However, I was not informed, and the executive producer claimed full credit for creating it. He never acknowledged that it had been my brainchild, or my sweat in front of and behind the camera. I was angry. That award could have helped to give me the connections to go forward with that work and touch many more children's lives.

Feeling ripped off, I quit working with that investor. I had to struggle for one and a half years to reach an understanding inside myself that holding onto a grudge built from anger and resentment hurt me, not him. I realized that in order to move on, I had to forgive him. I had always thought forgiveness meant reconnecting, but I came to understand that I didn't necessarily have to talk it out with him. I could forgive in my heart. Big lesson. Forgiving the whole thing freed me, and I was able to be grateful for all I experienced and learned through that television series.

When coming to terms with forgiveness, images of my childhood came to mind. I remembered being called

"Uglystick," and recognized that I still carried toxins inside of me. I forgave those children, and felt compassion for them. I saw how people who are cruel are unhappy, and in an attempt to feel better, project their own pain onto someone else. I transformed my past, healed myself in the present, and was now free to create a brighter future. Blame could no longer claim my power.

In addition to momhood, becoming a newspaper columnist, facilitating workshops, speaking to groups, and writing books kept me busy.

"Train children not by compulsion but as if they were playing."

~ PLATO

"Educating the mind without educating the heart is no education at all."

~ ARISTOTLE

CHAPTER 17

Sowing Seeds of Understanding

In Kansas, my daughter attended three years of public school. I spent a great deal of time in meetings trying to bring healthy changes to the school system. Then, when she was in third grade, she was assaulted by some boys on a bus. They said they were "just teasing" her. Her concussion seemed like anything but teasing. The boys were forced to apologize and kept home from school for two days.

I was livid that the situation was handled in such a cursory, incomplete way. By that time, my reputation had grown, as TV host, radio personality, and writer of the newspaper column "Kids 'n Stress." Leaning on that reputation, I met with school district administration, teachers, counselors, and the principal to be okayed to facilitate a session with the boys and my daughter. Finally, after hours and hours of meetings, permission was granted. Two teachers would be there, and the boys' parents were invited to come. (None of them did.)

On a table in a small conference room, I set up art supplies, which included a sheet with a body outline to fill in, at four places—three for the assaulting boys and one for my daughter. When the boys entered, my daughter was already sitting at the table. They would not look at her. It was a clear demonstration of the poor value of forced apologies.

The boys were nervous. I greeted them in a friendly tone, invited them to sit down, and said, "We are not going to talk. I just want you to color right now." They look puzzled. I explained. "These body outlines represent what you felt the day you hurt Erin on the bus. She is going to color how she felt inside herself, and you can do the same." They looked at each other as if to say, *What is* this? But they began to color.

After a few minutes, one of the boys raised his head, looked at my daughter, and said, "I am so sorry for hurting you." His eyes, tone of voice, and body language looked present and sincere. The other two boys stopped coloring, looked at Erin, and gave heartfelt apologies. She accepted. I asked them to share what they colored inside their body outlines and to explain what they were feeling when they hurt her. Their coloring was filled with darkness and jagged angles. One boy's heart area had a morbid face in it. My daughter's coloring showed "X" in areas where she got physically harmed and where she felt afraid and sad, using gray and brown colors. After they took turns, my daughter shared what it felt like to be assaulted. They apologized again. There was no more avoidance and discomfort at school with any of them.

CHAPTER 18

Westward Ho and Home Schooling

Oregon and its enticing natural wonders beckoned in 1985, and we moved there. I decided that instead of continuing to try to change the way schools manage education, it would be more efficient to homeschool my kids. Schools offered education in basic subjects, but where was the focus on the spirit and the learning style of the individual? I believed in whole-body learning, individual style and pace, and helping children to know their purpose by studying what they were interested in. Taking full responsibility for their education was going to be a huge challenge and would take all the self-discipline I had. Scared out of my wits, I put together curricula that were creative and custom-tailored.

Mornings were for custom-tailored learning experiences. In the afternoons, they devoured books and worked on projects that covered subjects they wanted to learn about. Switching to being teacher and students was not always easy. Sometimes, instead of calling me Mom during school hours, they took it upon themselves to change my name. One of their favorites was Mrs. Pee-Boots. (I loved taking them to the forest, and I had to take leaks there often, and my boots took on…damage.)

My daughter, Erin, at the age of twelve, initiated a project where she wrote over eighty letters to companies that were practicing animal cruelty. When the responses rolled in, she told me, "Those companies use different words but are all saying the same things. They are trying to make it look like they don't practice animal cruelty, but they do. The only way to get them to stop is to change laws." I applauded her both for what she did and for seeing through the language.

My son, Darion, at the age of nine, wanted to have his own office supply business. He gathered free items like stickers, pencils, writing pads from giveaways at stores and wrote away for free samples. He kept tabs on spending and profits in a special book. He created advertisement flyers and bags to give free with purchases. And, of course, anyone who visited our home was invited to his room to make purchases.

All along, one of my primary goals was to keep their imagination and inner child enlivened. My previous creative work in teaching many children how their minds, bodies, and emotions work together became part of my homeschooling curriculum. I taught my kids self-calming techniques and they used body outlines and communication skills to resolve sibling rivalry. It all took a lot of time.

For history, I used guided imagery in history. My favorite class, though, was experiential anatomy. We drew pictures of body parts and their functions, colored the pictures, pinned them on our clothing, and acted out their function in creative ways. The best one was when my son was the epiglottis and I agreed to act as chewed-up food. Apparently, I kept going down the wrong pipe, and umpteen times he "spat me out" onto the pillows we kept restacking to catch my landings.

I wanted them to function with deeper layers of understanding, and used fun, creative projects to help their brain development. For example, designing and making clothes or a stuffed doll instead of just buying these things off the shelf. Part of the goal was to teach them appreciation for the work that went into making things, instead of taking them for granted.

Each spring, I arranged a field trip to the public school, where my kids each spent a day in a classroom of their grade level. At the end of the day, each of them were asked to choose what they wanted to do the following school year: continue to be homeschooled or go to the public school. For any significant growth, they had to exercise their own wills and take responsibility for their choices. Each year, they chose homeschooling, saying it was more efficient. For high school, they enrolled in the accredited correspondence American High School.

The kids decided they would speak up when they needed socialization. They talked about quality contact. Their friends loved coming to our house. I always had fun activities at what was referred to as my Camp Run-A-Muck. My parents, at first opposed to homeschooling, observed results they respected and were glad I had the courage to do it. There was no paycheck for this hard work.

My children were more important than anything else. But I also wanted to help other children. In 1987, I marched on Capitol Hill in an attempt to improve education for children. With a flyer entitled, "The Fourth R" in hand, I walked into every single office on Capitol Hill. I delivered my seedling ideas for change in education. "The Fourth R" stood for readin', ritin', 'rithmetic, and relaxation. I knew children would benefit from learning relaxation skills in the academic setting. I never heard back from any of the politicians. Some people said that what I was seeking was too idealistic for education.

Countless times I have been told in brash tones that I am too idealistic, too optimistic, too hedonistic, and live in La-La Land. Saving myself punishment from being a "sassy smart mouth," I refrained from inviting others to join me in La-La Land. I am anchored in everyday reality—I just blend it with fun and positivity. For the last fourteen years, I have worn glitter every day to bring sparkles to the world in honor of children. The sparkles remind me to keep my inner child alive.

CHAPTER 19

My Medicine Wheel

Under the influence of mentors and teachers, and special practices, movies, workshops, and books from all over the world, my spirituality continued to grow. I saw that my own spirituality was a significant part of my human potential. I wanted time and ways to explore the spirit of life, and I built an eclectic Medicine Wheel in the forest that honored every philosophy or religion that had touched my growth, including Catholicism, Buddhism, Taoism, Native American spirituality, and others.

At the Medicine Wheel I awakened to the true meaning of being grounded. Among other techniques, I learned to breathe from the Earth and into my feet with beautiful light. Getting grounded was helpful for my active ADHD brain functioning.

One technique came to me through serendipity. I went to a hot springs where there was a caretaker, Mary Ann. When I got there, I gave Mary Ann homemade muffins. We ate one and started talking about the Earth's precious resources. That conversation about honoring the Earth Mother was a sign to Mary Ann. Her eyes got big. "You're the one." She told me about a Native American medicine woman who had been there the day before. She taught Mary Ann a chant, and told her to expect a woman that would give her a sign she was the one to pass it on to. The medicine woman said this woman would use the chant for the good of the Earth. I was surprised to have been "seen," and was touched to have been chosen.

Mary Ann taught me the chant, which was used to connect with the Earth. TOE HUM CUM RA. She said it is the sound of the Earth Mother's heart becoming one with our hearts, breathing together. We chanted it together, slowly inhaling with the TOE HUM, exhaling with CUM RA. Several rounds of this chant created within me a new appreciation of what it meant to connect with the Earth and feel grounded. It became something I used with many of the people I work with.

Nature, with all its magic and serenity, is the greatest healer. The Medicine Wheel provided sacred space for my own growth and the growth and healing of many others as we worked in multi-dimensional ways.

It is an honor and privilege to be trusted and help others on their journeys. Over a span of almost thirty years, Maya Brachmann trusted me with being an inspirational catalyst, many times at the Medicine Wheel, to assist her with spiritual and psychological breakthroughs. The combination of the messages coming through me and the energy of nature's healing culminated in Maya gathering more of her own innate abilities for managing major life changes and gave her the courage to take her life in a new direction. Similarly, Michelle Nowak attended many of my workshops, classes, and private sessions to further her spiritual growth and wisely integrated into her daily life what she learned. At the Medicine Wheel, a number of times she experienced nature's signs coinciding with her insights and breakthroughs. By valuing herself, building relationships, and seeking higher ground in the spiritual realm, she opened herself to many self-healing tools.

Seeking ways to support a vibrant energy as I age, I took a Qi Gong class. I learned about cleansing and toning my internal organs every morning. I also learned how to introduce others who cannot see it to sense to their own energy. (Hold two hands about a quarter of an inch apart, palms facing, fingers lined up. Hold still and breathe slowly. Wait until the fingertips feel warm or start to tingle. That's your energy.) All ages have enjoyed learning this simple technique.

I have observed what happens energetically when people laugh. I use it in healing work. It creates such a positive atmosphere that I've wondered why laughter wasn't a part of school curriculum. I started to use laughter in the Self-Healing classes and the Prevention classes for teaching self-help skills to children I taught at the University of Oregon. When a group of people laughs heartily together, it is a powerful release and aids in communing with one another.

Fun and play are fundamental and fuel my inner child. Dress-ups, jokes, and being silly are all part of my life. My purse always has unusual contents. I am not ever without my magic singing wand.

"Imagination is more
important than knowledge."

~ ALBERT EINSTEIN

CHAPTER 20

Expanding My Work with Children and Teens

After homeschooling my children for eight years, I began to work for Options Counseling in Eugene, Oregon, and was stationed at Bohemia Elementary in Cottage Grove. I worked with low-income students. I was given the most challenging cases because my 3-D learning approach was successful. The children seemed to love my office space in the gym, where we used dress-ups and they could act out their troubles with toys, art supplies, drums, and a singing crystal bowl. I discovered that whenever I used the crystal bowl during a session, there was usually a breakthrough. (I researched it and learned that crystalline sounds massage the listener at the cellular level, causing release and change in the cells.) The principal was concerned about me doing home visits because of the potential danger of walking into unstable situations. I used my intuition. And I baked goodies to take to homes that might not be receptive to a therapist knocking on the door.

One day, the principal, a counselor, and the janitor knocked at my door. They were restraining a suicidal third grader. He was not on my list of clients, but the situation was urgent. They brought him into the office, left, and closed the door. There we were, the suicidal boy and me.

By then I had developed a method of asking for quick spiritual guidance in my work. Over time what I discovered was that if I followed the pictures and messages I received, success would occur—and I was not to question the guidance. I learned that if I didn't follow through, the results were not as successful. This situation was urgent. When I asked for guidance, the message I received surprised me. It suggested I have a belching contest with this angry boy. Looking at this poor child who wanted to destroy himself, I said in a compassionate tone, "I bet you are really tired of all this serious stuff. Do you see those shelves across the room? Those are all prizes. How about we have a belching contest? Whoever wins gets to pick out a prize." The boy's head moved back in with a surprised look on his face. His shoulders dropped an inch as if he was relieved. He readily agreed.

In those days, my belches were pretty good. I could even belch my name, but it was going to take me a minute to muster up the gas, so I invited him to start. He let out a whopper. Then I let out a whopper. We decided to hold ten rounds, with the winner being the one who let out the most whoppers. His whole body got into champion form and his efforts were noteworthy. The room started to smell, but I didn't say anything. He won and excitedly went to the prize shelves. He took his time and, when he found his prize, he came back, half smiling. He sat in a chair and started talking, and talking, and talking. He released, and came to grips with his situation, one he had not voiced to anyone. Fun was a critical factor in his healing.

His parents were druggies and his grandpa was raising him. His grandpa became ill and had started talking about killing himself. Loaded guns were kept in a cabinet in the house. This boy was afraid he would have no family to take care of him, so he wanted to die before his grandpa committed suicide. Authorities were able to remove the guns from his grandpa's home. The boy and his grandpa continued to live together, helping each other. Belching helped to save two lives.

At this point, I also worked in an alternative high school with troubled teens who were unable to make it in regular classrooms. These young people knew more about sex, drugs, and violence than I ever did. Some carried weapons under their clothing. The alternative school itself was in a dark, dank basement. Determined to do what I could, I brought in my drums, and in every session we used drumming to bring out their emotions and release tension. I also brought in my biofeedback instruments and lots of visual aids to help teach them about themselves and the results their everyday choices were creating. My sense was that they were hungry for something that would help.

One day, two male students got into a tense argument about a girl, blaming each other for something. I saw a knife sticking out of one sock. As they created a cross-fire of yelling and blame, I grabbed two biofeedback temperature trainers and, while they yelled, I clipped the leads onto their fingers. The instruments began to register that their hand temperatures were dropping. I pointed to the machines. "This is what you're doing!" They stopped arguing and looked. I explained that their emotions and actions were causing their hand temperatures to drop because of the tension they were both creating. I told them they could control what happened *inside* of their bodies by paying attention to their minds and emotions. The machines had their attention. They both stopped fighting and watched the machines respond. They started to intentionally modulate their emotions, their inner worlds, and observe the results on the machines. In my book, it was nothing short of a miracle watching these two young men learn to take control of themselves. With more practice with the machines, they gained awareness, maturity, and confidence in themselves. And that day, what could have been a tragic event was prevented.

Because of budget cuts, I had to leave my post at the alternative high school. On my last day, they bought me a cake. After I left, they boycotted. I was deeply touched.

Eventually, I moved on to do prevention work in the Drain, Oregon, elementary school. My program ran for several years, thanks to funding from grants and philanthropic sources. It was a true village approach. Cow Creek Seven Feathers Foundation, U.S. Bank, and other organizations funded the holistic program I designed.

Initially, Cassie Ruud's mom, Sharon, the head teacher at the high school did not like what I was doing. She considered my classes too "touchy-feely." However, her kindergarten-age daughter's behaviors began to improve dramatically, bringing great relief to the family. Before then, they had feared their daughter, Cassie, was destined to be a troubled teenager. Her mom grew to respect what I was doing and nominated my program for an award from the State of Oregon for most innovative program developed from the ground up. Cassie, now an amazing young woman, sometimes speaks to my classes at the University of Oregon. She says my program gave her a new life.

My program consisted of spending time with 113 children in grades K-3 for forty-five minutes a week. Each week we covered a feeling theme, such as anger, sadness, jealousy, stress. They would be given a body outline to color and note where they felt the tension or sensation in their bodies connected to the feeling we were talking about. I showed them how the mind, body and emotions worked together. Every child received a parent newsletter with tips on home reinforcement for each topic. Teachers received a page of ideas for classroom integration and reinforcement.

Once a month, at the community center, I provided free parent training about the four topics I had covered with the kids that month. I wrote a weekly column in the newspaper about the importance of that week's theme. Included in the article were students' names and examples of their successes in using the skills they learned. Every month, the children each received a recording to take home of a story on each topic that incorporated the high points of the themes covered that month. In addition, the children were encouraged to share their success stories out loud with the other children.

Some parents were violently against the program. I was yelled at, shunned by some parents, and even received death threats. As I did at Teen Outreach, I kept a steady pace and did not quit. They didn't understand that prevention skills would reduce stress and improve relationships. Sometimes self-help skills can save lives.

One little boy I will call Rob never shared a success story in the three years I had been teaching. I knew he was troubled. Finally, one day he raised his hand to share his success story. He said on Saturday night he was on a bridge with his parents. They got into a bad fight, forgot he was there, and accidentally knocked him off the bridge. He grabbed a tree limb hanging over the river. He was scared. It was a winter night, dark and cold. "I remembered the song you taught us last week, Janai, and then I knew what to do." The song we had marched and drummed to was, "Breathe, Think, and Make a Good Choice." Rob said he took a deep breath, thought, and was able to make a good choice. He figured out how to get himself to safety on the shore. Unlike the time I had been frozen in fear when I was face to face with the copperhead snake in the basement, this little second grader empowered himself to save his own life. Even though he could not control his outer world, he still had control of his inner world.

CHAPTER 21

Teaching Children, Teachers, and Parents in Peru

I was hired to teach my program at an International School in Lima, Peru, for one week. The US Embassy also asked me to train their health department employees in the latter part of the week. The staff at the school, the parents, and the students all were so enthusiastic. I was treated like a rock star. It was an honor. It was odd to have to leave the US, a country I thought of as bold and innovative, in order find the enthusiasm for and belief in developing skills to expand our potential.

People from other schools in Lima heard great things from the teachers and parents of the school where I was teaching. Some teachers from other schools asked to attend the sessions. Great success stories arose quickly from the participants at the Lima International School. Their receptivity to what I taught greatly exceeded my expectations.

It was such a thrill and privilege to be trusted with their time and energy. The principal of the school reported that attendance during my week of training broke all previous records of teacher and parent participation. The success filled my heart, and this powerful week in Peru was a great milestone in my career.

CHAPTER 22

Change in the Wind

Grantors changed their funding focus, which brought my wonderful program to an end in Drain, Oregon, so I sought ways to reach children once again through television. Two women from the Southwest contacted me and arranged for Shari Lewis and Lamb Chop's booker to come to my house for several days, where I hosted them and demonstrated my techniques for children. They handed me a contract to produce a national television series with me as host, creator, and co-producer. The contract was deficient, so I could not sign it immediately. That was fortunate. An intuitive feeling kept tugging at my heart and stomach. Something didn't feel right.

After they left, I began doing research. I discovered the executive producer and funder of the proposed series was making her money in a way I didn't want to be associated with. She was selling a video of actual executions and murders, and it was making the rounds with gangs. I withdrew from the project. After my creative juices had been flowing so smoothly, depression set in.

A Japanese company wanted me to write a book for young teens. They had been pursuing me for many months while I pursued the television work. I finally agreed to write a fiction novel. Their plans involved producing an animated feature film based on the book. The process of writing *The Secrets Inside Copper Mountain* was magical. For example, one day I wrote a scene about a river island. Then, to take a break and clear my head, I went on a hike, and stumbled into a place that looked like what I had just written about. Shivers ran through my body. The book was published the same week the Japanese company collapsed financially. No film feature. No budget for marketing. They gave me all rights to the book.

In the following years, I wrote more books for children and adults, but marketing has been my downfall. I was honored that Goldie Hawn's foundation chose some of my books for children to be on their website as resources for parents and teachers.

CHAPTER 23

Peak Experience in the Wild

It was April of the last year I would be working at the Drain, Oregon, Elementary School and the week of my fifty-fourth birthday. I wanted a gift from nature for my birthday. I went for a walk up the mountain. I walked up a steep incline on a dirt logging road and reached the small plateau at the top. I stopped, and there, not fifteen yards in front of me, was a wildcat. It looked to be sniffing, hunting for food. He did not see me behind him. A lightning bolt of fear shot from my feet through my head. I was downwind, so he could not smell my fear.

I knew I had to make a choice, and quickly. Either I could quietly back down the mountain, or I could stay and follow the wildcat. If I stayed, fear could play no part in this. I chose to stay and release my fear.

Quietly, slowly, I bent to pick up a stick. They say that if a wild animal sees you waving a stick slowly above your head, it makes you appear larger than it. It was my safety stick.

The wildcat started to walk away slowly. I kept pace, walking when he did, and followed him for a few minutes. Then he turned and went into a grassy meadow. I walked to the edge of the meadow and waited. Suddenly the wildcat jumped into the air and pounced into some tall grass. He stood, and turned his head. He had a mouse in his mouth.

Then our eyes locked. We stood, motionless, for a good three to four minutes. Then he started to move in *slow* motion, lowering his back end to the ground. Then he *slowly* lowered his chest and head, keeping his eyes high enough to see over the tall grass. The entire time, his eyes were locked on mine.

My inner voice told me to follow suit. In what seemed to my leg muscles to take an eternity, I *slowly* lowered my back end, then *slowly* lowered my front end, until I was in the same position. Our eyes remained locked.

We stayed put. After several minutes my legs begged me to stand up. Going as slowly as I had before, I raised myself up in the same way. When I was again standing, the wildcat copied me, keeping the mouse in his mouth. Our eyes were still locked.

Finally, I decided to speak to him. I said out loud, "Hi. I am Janai. I am so very grateful you have shared this special experience for my birthday. Thank you from my heart." He seemed to be listening. "My work is for the children in the world, including the children of nature, like yours. Today I want to see if the irises are blooming. I ask for safe passage to the iris field."

When I finished the word "field," he looked away, turned slowly, and walked up the side of the mountain, with the mouse still hanging from his mouth.

I was filled with an ecstatic energy, a state of grace and gratitude. Once again, my human potential had expanded beyond what I could have imagined.

"Kindness heals."

~ JANAI MESTROVICH

CHAPTER 24

Broken Leg and Self-healing

In my garden, I was holding a basket in the crook of my left arm and a sharp knife for clipping vegetables in my right hand, I turned quickly, forgetting I was standing next to an irrigation pipe. My left foot got trapped and I fell to the ground, causing multiple spiral breaks in my leg and a smashed heel.

I was encased in solid white light, save for two little dots. There was no way to know how long I lay there. At some point, I knew I was supposed to choose the dot on the right. Then I woke.

When I tried to move, I was shocked to see that my foot was not correctly connected to my leg. I had to pick it up and hold it or it just dangled. "How could this happen? Why did it happen?" An inner locution voice spoke. *Stop what you are doing. Deal with the situation right now.*

My mind switched directions, I began breathing slowly and feeling grateful, knowing it was key to keep energy flowing instead of being fear-blocked. I screamed for help. My husband finally heard me, got me to the car, and we headed to the hospital.

On the ride I tried to allow only grateful thoughts to fill my mind: Grateful to be alive. Grateful to live at a time when there are cars. Grateful to be a mom. Grateful there was a hospital thirty minutes away, and so on. I dedicated the experience to helping others in the future with whatever I would learn.

The X-rays showed several spiral breaks and a smashed heel. Surgery was set for the next day. A splint was placed on my leg, and since there was nothing else that could be done before surgery, I was sent home. I took no pain meds. It was a strange experience to feel the disconnection between my foot and leg. I could feel that the foot did not move in conjunction with the leg. It dangled. I felt the pain, which was intense, but again, I did not translate the pain as "ouch." Instead, I continued to feel grateful, which is my foundation for healing. I also used visualization, affirmations, and keeping my attitude positive, certain that I would heal.

Meeting the doctor before surgery, still keeping an attitude of gratitude, I said, "Thank you for your work. I trust you. My life will be better because of your caring and thoroughness." He looked into my eyes, shook my hand.

A titanium rod and four screws were implanted from the knee to the ankle while I was under general anesthesia. I could not move my leg more than a quarter of an inch at a time for a long time after surgery. The first day I visualized all the cells in my leg having a welcoming party for the "new neighbor" who was moving in. I held a grateful feeling for this new titanium rod. In my mind's visualization, we all had tea, laughs, and an all-around good time. It felt like a celebration.

I Love Lucy videos became my fun-fix to create endorphins. Through books and teleconferences, I learned more about self-healing. I tried one of the energy techniques on our dying cat, who had not eaten for three days. At sixteen, he was on his way out. When I used the healing technique that combined visualizing him living and being filled with golden light while creating an energy circuit with my hands around him, he began eating and walking, back to normal in no time at all. He lived five more years.

Seeing the energy work provide life for my cat, I began using a variety of techniques on my leg—visualizations, chanting, using my hands and focusing golden light on the leg. Research had proven that the purring of cats helped bones to heal, so I visualized millions of cats purring into my leg several times daily. Most of all, I used my will. I allowed no thoughts of fear, worry, doubt, or negative images. My goal was to dance again. The surgeon said my left leg would not be able to do everything exactly like my right leg. I refused to believe that diagnosis. My choice was to *not* be a worrywart, like my mom. I wanted to go beyond my genetics. I knew worrying would take energy away from my healing. I chose to paint my reality on the open sky.

My efforts proved successful. I did not even go to physical therapy. The surgeon looked at follow-up X-rays and determined I could be released two months earlier from his care than planned. He leaned back, looked at my leg and said, "If I were going to write a book, I would put you on the cover for what you have accomplished."

"I am what I think.
I create my own reality."

~ JANAI MESTROVICH

CHAPTER 25

Pain Control

Throughout my adult life I have worked with pain control. As I grew older, I requested no pain meds before, during, or after bunion surgery. Dr. Melissa Monson, who performed the hour and twenty-five minute surgery, said she would never forget that day the rest of her life. The dentist who pulled my first tooth and did the implant said that my abilities in the procedures gave him hope for the human race. And he charged me only half the cost. In the past few years I have had two more teeth pulled and two more implants where a pin is screwed into my jawbone. Dr. Frank Stroud has performed two of these implant procedures where I requested no medication for any part of the tooth-pulling surgery or the implant processes. In one situation there was abscess to deal with, requiring more time for me to focus in the dental chair. Last year a doctor who has a pain clinic and teaches dentists how to do implants heard about my efforts. He videotaped an interview, took pictures, and asked how I do it. He now uses the video in his classes.

My approach with pain of the mind, body, emotions, or spirit is to use it as a signal to practice self-help skills whenever possible. Johanna Joyner has been a mentor for over fifteen years. She has taught me that the light is not at the end of the tunnel; it is *in* the tunnel. Pain control requires determination to find ways to light the way out of pain's tunnel.

CHAPTER 26

Heart Murmur

At this year's annual physical, I told my doctor that I wanted to start doing self-healing visualization on the heart murmur I contracted when I had rheumatic fever in first grade. Being invested in alternative healing methods herself, she understood what I was saying. But she had a concern.

"There can be different causes for a heart murmur. Before you start visualizing, I want you to have an ultrasound to see what that cause is. Then you can visualize appropriately." She listened to my heart and thought she heard something. One week later, I was at the hospital having an ultrasound. The technician knew why I was there and she looked at my heart from every angle. After a few minutes, she stopped, looked at me, and asked, "What are you doing? Your heart is so strong. It looks great and is beautiful. People your age usually have extra tissue or other obstructions that cloud what I see, but you don't. In fact, your heart looks stronger than most." I told her about the many self-help techniques, from positive affirmations to Qi Gong and more, that I have been using for decades

"I think what your doctor heard was just the sound of the blood being pumped in such a strong heart. You have no murmur."

Then she asked permission to take a look at my liver. She was curious. I agreed. After scanning around, she beamed. "Your liver is so clean. It's as beautiful as your heart."

Having this information felt like a gift from the heavens. It felt amazing to learn I had inadvertently healed my heart murmur.

Before I left, the technician asked me, "What do you consider the most important factor that may have healed your heart murmur?" I was happy to share. "I think all the self-help practices play a role in it. The most important is my positive attitude. I keep gratitude in my attitude." She smiled as big as you please. She got it.

I have done so many things for my health overall, I thought that maybe the heart murmur was healed as part of those efforts. I also wonder: Because I am so interested in learning more about what my potential is, perhaps the potential itself grows, and even more becomes possible. The mind and body are so incredible that I keep asking *What if?* And I remember to feel grateful for what is.

CHAPTER 27

More Deaths

In the 1970s, Dad contracted emphysema from a life of smoking an average of two to three packs of cigarettes a day. Doctors gave him five years to live. He decided that was not a good prognosis. Despite physical setbacks, by sheer willpower he made it to the age of seventy-nine, and died in 1998.

He did not talk about the tragic parts of his experiences in World War II until he was nearing his death. He told bone-chilling tales of seeing snipers when he was alone in the forest and fearing for his life. Knowing it was kill or be killed, he had to pick up and use his gun. Worse, though, was when he was hidden by a poor farming family in China. They risked their lives by hiding him underneath their humble abode. Japanese soldiers came in looking for American soldiers, and jabbed their bayonets through the floorboard. He was spared both injury and capture, thanks to those good people. I began to understand more of what he had kept inside that had created unrest in his heart. It opened my mind to understand him and his ways when I was growing up.

The night Dad died, his spirit came to me. I knew he was there; his energy was strong. He told me it was time. That next morning, I received a call that he had died. I had a contract with a video game company to do a series of stress management classes to prepare them for crunch time. That morning I was to facilitate the fifth class. I knew Dad would want me to do my work.

All morning I taught the employees, not telling them until the end of the class that my dad had died. Once again, my will and skill carried me through a challenge. I knew Dad would be proud of me—my feelings were not worn on my sleeve that day.

Nineteen ninety-nine brought the early death of the youngest in our family, my brother Johnny. He was thirty-seven. When he was twelve, Johnny had been introduced to drug use by his baseball coach. (When my dad learned this many years later, he swore if he ever saw that coach he would kill him.) Johnny became a regular substance abuser. He was so bright, so cute, and had great talent as a musician and philosopher, but he squandered his life energy. He had admitted to getting so desperate that he sometimes resorted to digging through trashcans for used needles and shared needles with other users.

Johnny's reality was hard for me to relate to. He did not have an easy relationship with Dad, and Mom had used his presence in her womb as a bargaining chip for new clothes. I provided much of his childcare. He and Mom had both good times and times of struggle in their relationship.

What Johnny needed growing up was consistent, consequence-based, tough love. But that was not something Mom and Dad could carry through with. As parents, they were unsure and afraid as they struggled to deal with Johnny's drugged life. My sister and I tried to help him when we could, but Johnny chose his own way, one that was hard to witness.

One evening he told me that he really liked the adrenalin rushes from the drugs and life on the edge. I wasn't sure what he meant. He explained. "There is a warrant out for my arrest in Missouri, but not in Kansas. The other night I put cocaine in my shirt pocket. When I got to Missouri, I purposely drove faster than the speed limit. The fear of getting caught speeding gave me a rush—I figured they'd be pretty tough on me if they also caught me with cocaine. But they didn't catch me." He was in deep trouble, and I so wanted to help him.

A week later, he showed up at my place at four in the morning. He said that the mafia was after him. He didn't share all the details, just that a drug deal went sour. Holy Mother Mary and Jesus Christ! I got the shivers. My children were young. Would the mafia actually burst into my home? Was my family in danger? Johnny started to nod off to sleep. He was in such a drugged state that I couldn't kick him out, and he was in no shape to drive, anyway. So I made sure the house was locked up and I kept watch on the street. As I kept fearful guard, I knew that this was not a reality I wanted to share.

Late the next morning when Johnny awoke, I explained it

was not appropriate to come hide at my house when the mafia was chasing him. My family was being endangered. I told him he could not return. I said I loved him and wished he would get help. He understood as much as he could in his drugged-out state. It was a sad moment.

When Johnny died, he was on three times the legal amount of methadone used for withdrawal. Prescription drugs as well as illegal substances were also found in his system. His heart finally gave out in a way that was akin to it blowing up. His life, and his end, such tragedy.

After he died, a strange thing happened that confirmed that energy cannot be killed but goes on in some form. My brother Ted headed over to Johnny's apartment to begin clearing things out. As he got out of his car, Johnny physically appeared to him. It scared the daylights out of Ted. Then Johnny spoke to Ted: "What the hell are you doing, fucker?" Johnny laughed, then disappeared.

I wish Johnny could have held on to the beauty he had in his soul instead of trading it for adrenalin rushes.

In 2004, Mom let go of life in stages. She had been a member of the Hemlock Society, which supports a person choosing to die when it feels appropriate to her. In Mom's last wish book, she indicated she did not want to be kept plugged into life with drugs and machines. She did not want an ugly, slow death. Her wish was not to come true.

She had great health insurance, which can be helpful, but also detrimental. Because her insurance covered costs, I witnessed her being kept alive, her wishes disrespected, and her body mistreated. Had it been in my power, I would have stopped the process and allowed her to die with dignity. Instead, she lived through the horrors cast upon her: wrong medications, hallucinations, falling out of bed, purple and black bruises all over her body, bedsores. She was not living; she was in a hellish limbo.

During her death process, I had been going back and forth to Florida. Since I had studied with a Tibetan lama about how to help a person have an easier death transition, I planned to stay to help her when the time came. However, one night I had a powerful directive dream. A surgeon with a huge, bright light on his forehead came to me and said, "You are not supposed to be here when she dies. Go home."

It didn't make sense. I could help her. I had been helping her with the spiritual side of things, and she loved it. However, the dream was strong and clear. Saying goodbye to her, it felt like my feet were stuck in cement and my body couldn't pull them out. Finally, I left, which was so hard, because I knew it was the last time I would be with her in this life.

Later it dawned on me that Mom and my brother Ted were to be together when she died. I had resolved my issues with her, as had my sister. But Mom and Ted had not come to resolution, according to what she shared with me. I can only hope that her dying process offered them both something to help heal their relationship.

I was back in Oregon the day Mom died. I heard a voice telling me to connect with her on the spiritual level, to wear the earrings she had given me and pray and chant for her. When she died, I knew it. I went to the forest and the Medicine Wheel, which she loved, and I felt her standing by me. I heard her voice speak to me on the inner planes. *Janai, I wish I could hold your hand and touch you.* I started crying. Through my tears, I spoke out loud to her. "Mom, now is the time we can touch each other with our hearts." She stayed for a while.

A few weeks later, Mom came to me in a dream and told me she wanted me to have the special wood box with the burned-in decorations I had given her decades ago. She had kept it on her dresser. She said Ted had it now. When I checked with him, he said it was in his possession. I told him Mom had wanted me to have it. He chose to keep it.

At Mom's funeral gathering, we did as she had requested and drummed for her. She had come out to see me in Oregon a few times and had loved drumming. When it was my turn to speak, I shared a magical experience Mom and I had had several years earlier. I called the story "Butterfly Magic."

The last time Mom visited in Oregon, we were walking to the lake, and a glowing yellow butterfly crossed our path. Mom stopped walking, and said to me quietly, "Stop. Watch this." She extended her arm full length in front of her. The butterfly, which had flown past us, turned and flew directly to her and landed on her hand. I knew we were in sacred space with a winged one who also knew that. I breathed in the pure, true magic of the moment.

As with my Croatian grandma, Mama, I was chosen to share in a secret Mom carried. Several years before she died, she told me that, starting at age four, she had been sexually abused every week for two years. It happened every Sunday afternoon during nap time with the minister. I could barely stand to hear her tell me. My grandmother and my mother both had been victims of sexual violation. How could this be? If I could have made a deal with God, I would have asked to do something to have those experiences erased from their lives.

Once I learned what had happened to her, many things about her began to make sense—her rigidity, her lack of information about how to educate us about sexuality, her flirtatious nature with men. She could become furious at the drop of a pin. Anger had been stored up all her life. She viewed herself with dissatisfaction. All this created in her psyche confusing dynamics. Lovable as she was to others, she had blockages to truly loving herself.

Mom was a character others found as unforgettable, charming, and funny. But others did not know the severity of her discontent. She was depressed often, sometimes suicidal. Even with her troubles, she managed to touch others deeply.

After she died, I discovered a fascinating fact. Her attending physician during her dying process was Dr. Wahl. Mom died at 3:30 p.m. When I found my birth certificate, I saw that the attending physician for my birth in Ames, Iowa, 1949, was Dr. Wahl. I was born at 3:30 a.m. Of course, they were not related, but it was a discovery that gave me goose bumps and made me recognize our spiritual connection. Mom is missed.

In 2008, my brother Ted was headed home, in central Florida, when his motorcycle hit something that caused it to be tossed into the air, flip, and fall back down on him. Witnesses saw him stand up after the crash, and slowly turn, looking around as if to see the world one last time. Then he lay down. He was rushed by ambulance to the hospital, where he died a short time later. His upper body had been crushed.

Like Johnny, Ted started with substance abuse in his pre-teen years. He was struggling with Dad and Mom, and with his siblings. He had stomach problems and other ailments. Life was troubling for him. In high school, he showed me a drawing. He said it was what he saw when he was high. It was a picture of flying demons. It gave me a clearer understanding of his troubled soul. I wanted that little boy I used to take care of to be happy. He managed to live a productive life, unlike Johnny.

After high school, Ted joined the Marines and served in the Vietnam War. When he got back, he didn't want to talk about what happened there. When I would gently ask, he would say, "You don't want to know anything about it."

Interestingly, whenever he was on drugs or alcohol, we had good conversations. In fact, even when there was tension between us, if his reality was altered, he was great to talk to. He would talk for hours.

Ted worked for a number of companies before being hired to teach classes in a prison to inmates on waste management and water-related topics. He had an excellent knowledge of water and waste management and provided good support for his family. He enjoyed his family—his wife, kids, grandkids. And he was in love with motorcycles. As far as he was concerned, wearing a helmet was out of the question. It would have ruined the experience for him.

When he died, my sister and I were on the phone. That was when he came to me, as others have, to indicate he was okay with death. His body had been giving him a lot of discomfort and he was glad to be free from it, even though he would miss his wife, children, and grandchildren. The next day, hoping to ease his journey forward, I chanted for him for four and a half hours. He let me know it was helpful.

His unrest and level of tension kept him in pain that perhaps no one understood. I was glad for him that his difficulties were released. His life had never been easy.

"Being honest may not get you many friends, but it'll always get you the right ones."

~ JOHN LENNON

"Without honesty we can never know what could have been."

~ JANAI MESTROVICH

CHAPTER 28

Divorce and Living Alone

Everything has an end, and after thirty-six years of marriage, it was time for my marriage to end and for me to live differently. I was sixty-two and had never lived alone. The prospect frightened me. I asked for guidance.

In a series of meditations, I began to see the inside of a living space—the colors on the wall, angles of the ceiling, where the windows were placed, and more. "Ashland" kept coming in very strong. I contacted a realtor and set up an appointment to find an apartment to rent. When we walked into the first place, I saw the images that had been coming in meditations. I rented it.

It was time to go into a cocoon to heal and reconfigure my life. I chose to not listen to any music or watch any TV for fifteen months. I wanted to make note of my thoughts, blockages, emotions, and spiritual development, and did not want that diluted by the distraction of external noise. So I lived in silence. I faced loneliness. Found my determination. Released toxicity. Sought clarity of purpose. Practiced techniques for self-healing. Sought self-love. Transformed my fear. And most of all, I tried to stay grateful and offered up my process as something to bring me more ways to help both myself and others.

The good fortune of having a grandson when I began living alone was that I was able to enter into a child's world, where I could be free. Grandma Boomhood was a rite of passage into a healthy aging process. That was my intention and attitude. Transforming difficult experiences from the past gave me the ability to be happy in the here and now. I am so grateful I gave myself that time in that cocoon. It was not easy. I went to hell and back multiple times. I kept telling myself that with all that powerful trauma blasting me, there must be a rewarding life waiting for me after I passed through the portal from hell. The lonely cocoon was key to setting up a wonderful third and final chapter in this life.

I see the past, present, and future dovetailing. My thriving inner child is youthening my spirit. I now want to know what my potential is as someone who's packing more years under her belt. I want to discover, have adventure, have joy, and play. I want to be *more* alive, not less. I don't want to feel dead in a living body. I am launching myself to be more alive at sixty-five.

As I adjusted to living alone, I used many survival tools. Baking up homemade goodies for people was pleasant and helpful. My Croatian grandmother, Mama, was right when she said, "If you are fortunate enough to have the ingredients to bake, always share, because it keeps you humble and grateful." It also helped me feel connected to people, like they were extended family. I reveled in taking cookies or bread to the woman who cleaned out the lint traps at the laundromat, which I came to refer to as the "loitering palace." She hugged me so hard the first time, I thought she was going to squeeze me to pieces. I kept an eye out for prospective recipients. It was important to feel connected to others. Baking and sharing does that.

A Zumba instructor, Sumara, inspired me with her style of happy exercise. My dancing spirit rejoiced in her classes. She asked me to be the poster girl for her fliers because of my style and energy. What unexpected fun to be a poster girl at sixty-two.

I did not seek a life partner to "save me" and "make me happy." To heal, I knew it was essential not to act out of a need, but to find happiness within myself. I am no longer afraid to live alone. I found contentment and happiness within my being. Self-love and respect are finally mine. Although the portal to find these life jewels was sometimes so intense I questioned if I would be all right, and the pain was almost too much at times, I made it through because of my strong will and skills. I remained grateful, positive, and kept open access to my joyful inner child. I "made lemonade," and have created a good life for myself.

When I teach at the University of Oregon, I provide a handout with huge letters for each student: I AM WHAT I THINK. I CREATE MY REALITY. It is a core truth that fuels the way I enrich my life. I work to practice what I preach. Human slip-ups are part of the deal, but I've developed hefty muscles from pulling up my bootstraps.

"Become as a little child."

~JESUS CHRIST

"I was wise enough to
never grow up while
fooling most people into
believing I had."

~ MARGARET MEAD

CHAPTER 29

Grandparenting Heaven

When my daughter told me that a child was on its way, I threw my hands in the air and screamed in delight. Another dream was coming true.

When my grandson finally arrived, I felt like I was flying on the wings of an eagle. Holding my precious little grandbaby and feeling that connection for the first time was a natural high. My daughter was a mother. And I was now a grandmother. A *grandmother!*

Even when Jackson was tiny, I would hold him up to my gong and chimes, take his little hand, and help him touch the musical instruments. His eyes filled with delight. We began drumming together before he was a toddler. When he first started to say words, he could not say "Grandma." But he was used to doing what we called "boom" on the drums. He started calling me "Boom." As he grew older and could say "Grandma," he started calling me, "Grandma Boom." That is how I got my grandma name. My two-year-old granddaughter shortened it for herself. She calls me "Boo." I love any name they call me. My grandies are special buds that help keep my inner child sparked. Their creativity keeps my mind stimulated, my heart full, my body active, and my spirit happy. The cross-generational connection is deeply meaningful. And healthy.

I long to have a positive impact on them. I hope they see that aging can be exciting, not boring and scary. And some day, if they have grandchildren, maybe they will remember special things to share that they enjoyed with me.

One of the most delightful things we do together is to turn on my toy piggy and doggie that roll on the floor and laugh. The three of us roll along with them. It's so funny. I have used those battery-operated animals when teaching a Self-Healing Tools class at the University of Oregon. The whole class roars with laughter.

The grandies and I have outrageous fun building pillow-blanket forts, doing dress-ups, drumming our feelings out, dancing crazily, marching and making up new songs, laughing at silly things that don't make sense, making messes baking together, toasting "Cheers!" with our forks, making faces and wearing silly glasses, crawling around like animals and making sounds, making up stories, learning that we don't touch bugs when we kiss them but keep a distance...and the list goes on.

Being with my grand little ones fuels creativity, spontaneity, adaptability, flexibility, and positivity. Those are "muscles" that strengthen and youthen my spirit. My grandies give to me as I am giving to them. We are both receiving. The bond is undeniable and fulfilling.

I have been able to help other grandparents realize that we are not the parents like we once were; we are *grand*parents. The role of a grandparent is different than that of a parent. We already had our chance to do things our way. Now it is our children's opportunity to figure out what they want to do in raising their children. Our job is to bond with the grandchildren, to be *fun*, and to respect the values and techniques practiced by the parents.

"What soap is to the body,
laughter is to the soul."

~YIDDISH PROVERB

"With the fearful strain
that is on me night and
day, if I did not laugh,
I should die."

~ABRAHAM LINCOLN

"I am thankful for laughter
except when milk comes out
of my nose."

~WOODY ALLEN

Chapter 30

Fun Getting Older

My spirit has maintained a theme of fun in my life, regardless of difficult circumstances. I do it in honor of the inner child. I love generating joy. It gives me life, strength, refreshment, and happiness. Sharing it with others heightens the joyful energy.

Many years ago, when I was feeling down, a friend called to tell me something good that had happened for her. As I joined her in the feeling of celebration, it dawned on me that doing so brought me out of my funk. It was her joy, not mine. But I shared in it and gained from feeling it. That's when I realized it's always good to share joy, no matter whose it is. Just feel it. Then it becomes yours, too.

When I lived in the forest, for fifteen years I held a monthly gathering for people to have fun playing on drums. People from all walks of life joined in, from school principal to accountant to teachers, authors, musicians, social workers, nurses, university professors, stay-at-home moms. Sometimes we dressed in costumes and masks. Other times, we wanted to dedicate the drumming to someone who was ill. Each drumming gathering developed its own personality. It was a sacred space where we could play and create together. It gave us a natural high and energized us.

Theme parties were a hit. One of my favorites was the Ugly Party. I got the idea because we were always wanting to look our best for each other. Lots of people showed up for that one. I enjoyed decorating with ugly supplies! With loads of laughter, we had ugly contests, even an ugly belching contest. I never heard so many ugly belches in my life. A woman won the prize—a toy toilet.

For the past few years, I have been going to Los Angeles for my birthday. My son is part of the gay community there, and I find the gay and lesbian community more fun to party with. I find it delightful that even though I am straight, they totally embrace me without discrimination. My son hosts my birthday in wonderful ways. I get to dress up in fantastic outfits and be treated to exceptional events. His friends make me feel very special. I love them.

Last year when Darion, his friends, and I were at a restaurant, Cloris Leachman approached. I asked for her autograph. She said only if I did a "shot" with her. I said I didn't drink. She said, "You will before the night is over if you want a photo with me." I had made a vow that I would have more fun adventures each year than the year before. So, I thought, what the heck. I had never done a shot before; I'd learn what it was like. Besides, I wanted a photo with hilarious Cloris.

She was proud of the fact that she had made ninety shots of a drink for the crew on a movie set with Henry Fonda. This was the drink she was planning to make for me. When we found a bar that was open, Cloris told the bartenders to stand aside, that she was going to make B-52s. All they had was double-shot glasses. Cloris directed me how to do the shot. Once I got the layers of liquors, all the way down to the Kahlua, in my mouth, she told me not to swallow. I had to hold it in my mouth for a bit. My mouth was so full that I was afraid I was going to lose it and spew it all over her. I prayed for it to stay in. Finally, she told me to swallow. After swallowing, I became hyper. I got my pictures with Cloris. I was talking non-stop, driving Darion crazy. He insisted I dance off the B-52. I danced heartily.

The next night we attended an event at the Gay and Lesbian Center that Lily Tomlin established in Los Angeles. Jane Fonda was being interviewed as a benefit to the center. Jane and Lily have been good friends for a long time, and both have been inspirational to me. Lily knew I would love a photo with her. Just as we were about to take the photo, someone scooped her away, and she turned back and called out that we would take the photo in a while, that she would not forget. She returned when she could and was so kind, like a long-lost aunt. She insisted we take more than one photo to be sure I got one I liked. Jane was always surrounded by a crowd. She has such a strong presence. Her strength is undeniable. She was also kind to allow a photo with me to be taken. I felt fortunate to attend and meet women who have been a great influence in my journey.

My sixty-fourth year started with a boom. Back in Ashland, I learned how to SUP (stand-up-paddleboard). What an amazing core exercise. Feeling the movement of the water and keeping my balance proved to be very meditative. I felt connected to the sky and water with an unexplainable freedom for my spirit.

Fun and play launched another year at my sixty-fifth birthday celebration in LA. Darion and I went to a play on Friday night, Charley had a party at his house on Saturday night, and a lot of friends came to a party at a restaurant on Sunday. The Sunday party was filmed for a television show. I wore gold wings and had packed supplies for fun activities and prizes so we could play games at the restaurant. Everyone let their inner children out to play. Indoor snowball fights with fake snowballs, a licorice-slurping contest, an M & M straw-sucking competition, and silly dress-ups had everyone happy and laughing. I got excited wondering what else would arise to keep the good times afloat.

A few weeks after my birthday in LA, my son's friends actually called *me* and asked me to participate in a surprise birthday they were planning for him. I was very touched that they wanted his mother to join. I was flabbergasted that they wanted me to be the big suprise. They wanted me to hide in a giant, glitter-blasted present box in the middle of the party. My son would open the box, and I would be the surprise. My son loves superheroes, so on top of that I would get to create and dress up as my own superhero.

Flights were expensive, but I thought, what the heck, when will I have this chance again? I bought the ticket, flew down with an armada of luggage filled with costume supplies, superhero decorations, toys, and homemade cookies. All the guys, who were in their thirties, were excited to see me.

I had created a costume for Super Grandma Boom: shiny turquoise wings and sequined top and tights, a multi-colored headpiece, seven inches tall, decorated feathers, jewels, and lights powered by two battery packs pinned to the top of my head.

Party time! I hid in the box as I heard the sixty people yell SURPRISE! My son slowly crept towards the box and started to open it. I burst out with enough flare to send everyone cheering. I will never forget the look of shock and surprise on his face. It took him several minutes to recover. Eventually, I got a "Mom.... MOM?!? What are you.... here.... What?!?" His reaction was priceless. It may be the only time that I saw him speechless.

Two years ago at Christmas, I decided I was tired of being sad every time my son left after his Christmas visits. We were at the airport when I suggested we take a fun photo he could post on Facebook. "Oh, Mom! It's too early in the morning."

"Darion, just trust me. This way we'll have something fun to end the visit with instead of being sad."

He reluctantly agreed. I got on the floor and acted like I was pulling his ankle to keep him from leaving. Now, taking a funny photo when he is leaving and we're at the airport has become a tradition. Last Christmas, I met Darion at the airport dressed up as the Christmas Fairy strung up in lights. What fun! I guess it wasn't such a bad idea to change sad to glad.

Recently, my sister's children were married one month apart. I helped with both weddings in other states. What joy to be a part of family celebrations, but it was also work. Karen and I were able to slip in "commercial *fun* breaks," where we would be silly. My brother-in-law, David, has astounding musical talent, and his harmonica, mandolin, and voice brought great fun to the mix.

One of my delights in Ashland is being in the parades. Last year, I won first place in adult entries as the Freedom Fairy. This year, I won second place. I wear beautiful wings and flap them as I run in a zigzag fashion from one side of the street to the other. I wave my wings over the children sitting on the curbs. It is a hefty exercise that brings great joy interacting with the crowd. And it takes a lot of energy!

CHAPTER 31

Living Alone Outtakes with My Patron Saint Lucille Ball

Note about Lucille Ball: She inspired me with her humor on the *I Love Lucy* show. I had never seen a woman caught up in so many funny predicaments, make so many funny faces, and still look attractive. There was no one like her. Sometimes I get into predicaments in my life that are not funny in the moment, but hysterical when I reflect on them. I always think of Lucy. It seems at times that she is my Guardian Angel or Patron Saint.

The dental assistant and the dentist both pulled away from me at the same time. The assistant exclaimed, "Janai, something flew out of your head and hit the doctor on his forehead!" They both looked shocked. The dentist looked down on the floor, stooped over, and picked up a bobby pin. He showed it to us. They were perplexed. They asked if that could have been what flew out of my head. A true confession ensued. "Yes, geez, I wear a wig." (It's the hair I always wanted. I just had to buy it!) "I put bobby pins on top of bobby pins, crisscrossed, in certain places to keep the wig in place. Sometimes a bobby pin is pinned so tight it acts like a canon and shoots out of my head. I am so sorry it hit you. I have no control over them." By this time, we were howling in laughter. After that, they kept glancing at my head in case there was another loose canon.

On another day, I was standing in line at the post office. When it was my turn, as I looked down to write a check, a bobby pin flew out, bouncing across the counter. The post-mistress looked stunned. "Janai, what WAS that? Something flew out of your head!" All the people standing in line stretched their necks to see what she was talking about. I explained the whole thing about the wig and flying crisscrossed bobby pins. Laughter filled the post office.

I Love Lucy strikes again...in my mouth, no less! I baked some deeelish cookies. I always lick the batter off the wooden spoon. I was in a hurry, ate a little batter, and placed bowl in the kitchen sink. I squirted some clear dishwashing soap into the bowl. Before I could run water into it, the phone rang. I finished the call and scurried back to the kitchen to take the cookies out of the oven. Then I turned to the sink and noticed the bowl with wooden spoon still had a good chunk of batter on it. I grabbed it and stuffed it into my mouth. *Oh gawwwwddddddd*...dish soap filled my mouth! Immediately, I spit and spewed into the sink. I turned on the faucet, filled my hand with water, and put it into my mouth to rinse. Perhaps it was a mistake to swish it around in my dish-soapy mouth. I began to lather. Zillions of miniature bubbles appeared. The more water and swishing, the more bubbles. I ate a few fresh hot cookies to destroy the taste of my internal cleanliness. It helped, but the cookies tasted so *clean*! Lucy, I always loved your shows. If there are remakes, can I audition?

Do you know what a fart finger is? Pull it and it makes a farting sound, a very *loud* farting sound. I keep one in my purse because my grandson gets such a kick out of it. One day, while waiting in the reception room of the dentist's office, I sat on my purse, which activated the fart finger. The receptionist and a patient in the room looked over at me with shocked expressions. "It was *not* me! Seriously, it was *not* me!" They looked incredulous, so to vindicate myself, I pulled out the fart finger and showed them. The receptionist insisted on pulling it. Then she showed me the fart app she kept on her phone for her young son! Who woulda thunk it. We now feel kindred in a quirky, fun kind of way.

My first apartment in Ashland had an infestation of flies. I was certain Lucy was with me—the flies were too fast for fly swatters and not attracted to the flypaper. In desperation, I bought a powerful vacuum. While the vacuum sucked them off the ceiling, the fan, and the windows, I was happily blessing the flies to a better life. Then I turned, and the powerful suction hose sucked two silk scarves off the back of my desk chair. And they didn't go through to the canister. They were stuck smack dab in the middle of the hose.

My cussing channel found the ON switch. I tried sticking a broom handle down the hose. As I prodded and probed, flies swarmed me. Probably mourning their sucked-up friends. A moment of joy? Not. Don't ask me why, but I happened to have a Native American arrow with arrowhead small enough to poke down the hose. After fifteen tedious minutes of trying, I accepted it wasn't going to work. Have I mentioned that it was eleven p.m.?

Maybe if I caught the edge of the silk scarves halfway through the hose, I could then pull them toward me and out. Joke was on me. Forty-five minutes later, I fell to my pillow hoping not to dream about swarming flies and stuck scarves. I reminded myself that I was teaching a class called Kids Solve Problems. Certainly I should be able to figure this out by myself.

Sunrise brought new ideas while the fly party continued. The tone was not my usual, *Here little buggies, I'll help you live outdoors,* but one of *You're in MY space and MY face, and you either get out or get sucked up...with blessings!* I spent the next thirty minutes working with a new tactic—slowly squeezing the hose to push the scarves toward one end—until my tired fingers begged for mercy. Google: Use suction from canister to pull things out of hose, little by little. Didn't work. Ugh. Totally joyless now.

OK. Next, combine techniques. Squeeze and push hose while using canister suction. Eureka! Slowly but surely—oh yes!—I got the first scarf out. A little shredded. Not too bad. In my jubilance and celebration at getting the first scarf out, I forgot to turn off the vacuum. I was wearing a long flannel nightie. The vacuum was sucking it up into the see-through canister and jerking me toward it. Ahhhhhh—fly karma! I pulled myself free and got second scarf suctioned and squeezed out. Distracted by success, once again I forgot to turn off the vacuum, and by the time I felt the tugging, half my nightie was flapping around inside the canister. Argh! Lucy got paid for doing this stuff.

Macho man and my cussing channel

I never used to switch on the cussing channel in my head until the year I got divorced and experienced a marathon of life crises. Now it turns on, mentally anyway, all-too easily, and I have to quell its fire by biting my tongue. One day at the loitering palace (laundromat) when I first moved to Ashland, I was putting my quarters into the washing machines, only to have the machines spit the quarters out across the floor. I tried everything from being gentle and slow to rapidly shoving one quarter on top of another to stay in the slot. After umpteen quarter-spits, the cussing channel in my head turned on. I already had the soap and laundry in the machines and didn't want to switch to other machines. I tried one more time. The machines spit out the quarters as if they were allergic to them and having a sneeze attack. I could feel Lucy's influence.

The man filling the washing machines next to mine was watching. I said aloud, "Either I'm going to cuss or laugh. Think I'll laugh." Just as I started laughing and popped another quarter in the machine, then watched it fly across the floor, Macho Man stepped into my territory and insisted I was not pushing the quarters *hard enough.* He offered to shove my quarters in for me. I resented being considered a softie-quarter-shover, but I was desperate for the machines to swallow silver.

With knuckled might, Macho Man shoved the first quarter in. Out it flew. Even farther than mine had. Probably because he was a heftier shover. I burst out laughing. He didn't. He retrieved the quarter and tried the second machine. Ching, Ching, Ching. The quarter bounced across the floor. By now my cussing channel was switched off, and I wiped laugh-tears from my face. That's when I realized I was dripping eyeliner. Macho man took several of my quarters and began shoving them one atop each other.

Spit, spew, sneeze, ching, ching. By now I was all but rolling on the lint-lined palace floor. Macho Man looked at my washer knobs. He said they didn't look like they were latched correctly. I'd never used this kind of machine before and thought I'd twisted the knobs all the way. Guess not. He didn't even have to use his macho-ness to turn the knobs a little bit in one direction, then try another quarter. Ta-DA! It worked. Relieved, I courteously bit my lip to stop laughing and thanked him. It really was nice of him to help, so I thanked him again, hoping the second thanks would make up for laughing at his attempts, and for having to look at my eyeliner-streaked face. I have never had so much fun at the palace.

A couple weeks after the quarter-spitting at the loitering palace, I had the beginnings of a sore throat. I Googled natural remedies and learned that one tablespoon of organic apple cider vinegar in a glass of water could help. Gargle, spit out. Gargle again, swallow. Repeat every hour. Meanwhile, I'd already put some baking soda in water to take to adjust the pH level in my body. So I drank some baking soda water and then chased it with apple cider vinegar, gargling and swallowing. *Holy Vesuvius!* My innards from my gut to my chest were making so many sounds that it sounded like a volcanic orchestra. Bubbly formations spewed up from my throat that were uncontrollable. Imagine what the activity *felt* like! Now I know how to make a volcano. And I got rid of the sore throat.

"I'm not funny.
What I am is brave."

~ LUCILLE BALL

CONFIDENCE IN ONESELF

Human potential is the same for all. Your feeling 'I am of no value', is wrong. Absolutely wrong. You are deceiving yourself.

We all have the power of thought~ so what are you lacking? If you have will power, then you can do anything. It is usually said that you are your own master.

~ H.H. THE XIVTH DALAI LAMA

CHAPTER 32

Special Grandma Boom Moments from My Journal

I received a call from my daughter, laughing and saying Jackson spoke to her about when he was in her tummy. "Mom, when I was in your tummy I didn't see Sissy anywhere in there!" Oh, to be inside a preschooler's mind.

Kristin was in her high chair and I'd just finished feeding her. She leaned forward, stretching her neck and head as close to me as possible and began to blink like a Morse code-in-a-baby machine. Blink. Blink. Blinkblinkblink. I leaned forward and returned the same blinking code. She smiled. I smiled. She blinked a new code. Grandma Boom answered it. After five rounds of blinking, she was finished communicating. Words are great, but human ingenuity comes up with so many other ways as well. It was a great way to connect.

Four-year-old Dr. Jackson, with the doctor kit he had received for Christmas, took my blood pressure. When I asked if he had any recommendations for me to feel good and healthy, he responded, "You will feel good if you play trains with me, Grandma." Heck, any Grandma Boom would go for a cheap, guaranteed natural prescription. It worked.

Crashing. I've never been drawn to it. However, I wanted to keep a fun connection with Jackson, who *loves* playing with trains and crashing them. I am an avid learner. While holding sweetie pie three-month-old Kristin, I came up with a new crashing game: count to three, then with gung-ho effort we both push our trains to crash in the middle. The crashing combinations were countless—off the tracks, on their tops, twisted over each other. I was amazed at how excited I got to see the new formations the crashes made. Jackson delighted in each and every crash as if it were the first time he had experienced this kind of thrill. It certainly was a new kind of "boom" for Grandma Boom!

My daughter called to say she'd been singing a song over and over, and Jackson approached her and said, "Mom, stop singing that song. It's stuck in my ear!" I find this stuff hilarious. They're so innocent, so literal.

"Keep them in your cheeks, Grammy," Jackson called to me from the top of the stairs as I was leaving.

"Keep *what* in my cheeks, Jackson?"

He smiled, pointed at his cheeks, puffed them out, and said brightly, "My kisses!"

"Your *kisses*?"

Excited, he said, "Yeah, Grammy, I keep all your kisses in my cheeks, so you keep all the kisses I give you in your cheeks."

I felt like we were part squirrel. I was happy to tell Jackson I would *always* keep *all* of his kisses in my cheeks. He agreed to do the same with mine.

I WILL... (I leaned my upper torso to the left.) ... I WILL (I leaned my upper torso to the right.) ... ROCK YOU (I nodded my head dramatically forward.) ... ROCK YOU (Head nodded dramatically forward and back again.) Repeat. Repeat. Repeat. Repeat. I was sitting in front of Kristin in her high chair. She had just finished eating. Perfect time to sing a simple jingle with body movements—captive audience. I did it slowly enough so she could follow and mimic me. She smiled and jiggled and made singing sounds that were nowhere near what I was saying, but a great baby-blend. When I stopped, she kept on. Music, happy faces, body movements are Grandma Boom and Kristin fun. WE WILL, WE WILL ... ROCK YOU!

Lucky Kristin, even though she was sick today. All she wanted was to be held for many hours. Whenever I put her down so I could do something, she was right back at my legs, begging to be held. I remember being sick and just wanting to be held too. It's a special kind of connecting that's different from normal days and activities. Even though my arms tired from carrying her so much, I knew I was fortunate. I was able to share love and caring for such a precious little one. It's a special Grandma Boom privilege that won't last long, because those little ones grow so very fast.

Sometimes ya just can't argue with a surprise answer. One morning I asked Jackson if he wanted more breakfast because he hadn't eaten very much. "No, Grandma, I'm full of kisses."

"But Jackson, you might need food for energy to play and feel good."

"No, Grandma, I'm full of kisses that feel good."

Jackson's daycare requires they make an accident report when a child falls or gets hurt. One day my daughter informed me that an accident report was sent home for three-year-old Jackson and his best friend, Jessie. They were hugging and fell down! LMAO. Would love a copy of that accident report to keep in my files!

One of the most precious, heart-touching moments happened with Jackson. The little guy was trying to keep his toys out of his crawling sister's reach. She kept crashing his toys with her walker.

When things got settled and she was napping, I got down on the floor at his level. I touched his face gently and looked into his eyes, and said softly, "Jackson, I really understand it is hard for you sometimes to share me with your sister. We had three years of just being buds with each other. I want you to know that I think about that and about how you feel."

He had been chewing a snack and had a runny nose. He stared at me for a few seconds, then without warning, opened his snack-filled mouth and plastered the biggest kiss on my cheek. He pulled back, looked in my eyes, then came forward again and gave me a second cheek kiss. Then he hugged me. He never said a word. The connection was deep and special.

Jackson had a glob of green play dough. I instructed him to use it to get his bad feelings out. After he worked the play dough, I asked him why he was holding his nose. He said, "Because good feelings smell good and bad feelings smell bad. I made a mountain of bad feelings come out of me and they smell really bad." After this release of his bad feelings, Jackson turned his attitude completely around. I told him how proud I was of him, that he had made a good choice to get those bad feelings out in a good way. He threw out his hands, dropped the green mountain of bad feelings onto the floor, grinned from ear to ear, and hugged me like there was no tomorrow. I was one happy Grandma Boom to have been a part of this transformation.

Today I practiced coo-vowels and coo-consonants with four-month-old Kristin. We stuck our tongues out at each other and made funny sounds. We both laughed. Then she made some coo intonations, some gentle (vowels), some strong (consonants). She would wait for me to respond in like. I simply mimicked her coo-vowels and coo-consonants with appropriate intonation and volume control. She got really good at guiding me through. I think she may have a strong handle on coo-storytelling. I do believe this girl is a talker!

"AWWWW, SISSSSSS! DISGUSTING! DISSSGUSSSTING! DISGUSTING! DISGUSTING! DISGUSTING! DISGUSTING! DISGUSTING! DISGUSTING! DISGUSTING!"

When I was feeding Kristin tonight, I counted nine *disgustings* in a row from Jackson. After taking on a full spoonful of squash and carrots, Miss Kristin chose to *blow* it out of her mouth with full force. Jackson watched it hit my face and spray my hair, neck, and shirt. She also messed up her bib, high-chair tray, and some toys. She laughed, I think maybe *at* me, not *with* me. It was hysterically funny. And Jackson was soooo grossed out. I'll never forget him looking at my squash-splattered face saying that word nine times. Priceless.

From the mouths of babes. I picked up Jackson and Kristin from daycare one afternoon. I was buckling Kristin into her car seat, when Jackson shouted to a passing gentleman in suit and tie: "Hi, little working man!"

The man smiled and asked me, "What did he say?"

I simply *could not* call him "little working man." I blurted out something like, "Oh, he's just being silly, saying things." The gentleman seemed content enough with that answer and turned and resumed his business-strut down the sidewalk.

As I climbed into the car trying to keep from busting a gut, Jackson asked me where the "little working man" was going. I had to turn on the Old MacDonald CD to get us off the subject so I could drive sanely.

How often do we stop to clap for ourselves? When Kristin was learning to walk, she would stand up, take some steps, then smile and clap. She reminded me that it's OK to be happy about ourselves.

A plastic image of Mickey Mouse decorated the tops of the cupcakes for Jackson's third birthday party at a venue where kids could engage in educational activities. It was eating time with fifteen preschoolers around a colorful table. I was feeding three-month-old Kristin and looked across the room just in time to see Jackson put a plastic Mickey Mouse in his mouth. He discovered it was a decoration, and not that tasty. He promptly removed the Mickey Mouse decoration from his mouth and put it directly back on the cupcake. I started laughing. What freedom!

In March of 2013 Jackson noticed a book at my house, *Farts from Around the World*. Ten countries, ten different fart sounds. He proceeded to push each country's button and tell me which family member or friend sounded like a certain sound. We laughed and laughed. On the other hand, when Kristin heard the fart sounds, she moved her little body like they were music to dance to. One country, in particular, had quite the fartistic flare with a fun dancing rhythm.

A couple of years ago when we were baking, Jackson insisted that we both pretend to be baby kitties and eat cookie batter. He showed me how: Place cookie dough on the kitchen counter, bend head down to the counter, and start lapping it up. Yes, I did it. Jackson was quite pleased that we were kitties together.

When Jackson was a toddler, his mom encouraged him to put his own socks on instead of getting help. He got frustrated when one toe would not go into the sock. In his irritation, he spoke directly to his toe, "Stop tricking me, toe!" Ya just gotta love such clear, direct body talk.

One winter morning, four-month-old sweetie pie Kristin learned the magic of sound going through her hand. I guided her hand to touch the side of the singing bowl, which I then "dinged" with the mallet. It creates a mesmerizing, peaceful, singing tone that fills the atmosphere. When a hand touches it, the sound retracts, becomes silent, and an amazing vibration runs through the hand and up the arm. Kristin only had to be shown once. After that, every time I "dinged" the bowl, she put her hand on it. She was loving her first science experiment! Happy baby girl and happy Grandma Boom.

Picture a three-year-old eating corn on the cob. He is chewing away, stops, begins to pick up each kernel of corn that has dropped onto his plate as he is chewing. He meticulously puts each dropped kernel back into a hole on the cob.

I could *not* resist asking, "Jackson, hon, why are you putting those pieces of corn back into the holes on the cob?"

He didn't even stop to look up at me when he said, "Because, Grandma Boom, they dropped off. I don't like to eat them off the plate. I like to eat them on the cob."

Well, there ya have it, folks.

"Grandma, you *have* to eat one of these. They were made for grammies." I didn't know what Jackson was talking about but called out, "OK, Jackson. What is it?" He appeared from behind the kitchen counter and handed me a "graham" cracker! Haha. I didn't really want one, but there was no way I would refuse a special cracker made for grammies.

After receiving the instruction from three-year-old Jackson, my daughter called one afternoon. He has a play cell phone. He had picked it up, taken it over to his mom, and said, "Call your mom." She obeyed. And we did have a few things to cover bases on. She laughed, explaining Jackson hears her tell her husband, "Call your mom," so he thought it was the proper thing to say. There's nothing like children reflecting back into their environment what has been shown to them.

Drumming our feelings. Frequently, Jackson, Kristin, and I drum our feelings out on a big drum I have. We practice drumming to different emotions because they all sound and feel differently. It's a great way for my grandies to begin playing with emotional intelligence activities that are *fun.*

"Sissy can't talk to you, Grandma Boom. She's eating her shoe!" That's what Jackson told me when we were pretending to call people on play phones. Then he told me to call her. So I called his sister, who was sitting right next to me. Of course, her mouth was too busy to carry on a discussion.

"Your body will tell you what it needs, Jackson. If you pay attention to how it feels, you will know if it has enough energy to do the whole tumbling class. If it feels too tired, listen to it, and tell me, and I can take you home." And so Jackson, who was having a bout with allergies, went into his tumbling group, enthusiastic and happy to be there. A little over halfway through, he came over to where I sat. He was droopy eyed and said he was too tired and wanted to go home. I commended him for listening to what his body needed.

Smiling as big as you please, eight-month-old Kristin was flapping her arms like they were chicken wings trying to fly. Why? Because she was excited to see me. She couldn't talk with words, so she talked with her body. Even though I have words, it felt so fun to flap my wings back to her and smile. *That* was peak communication.

"The itsy bitsy spider went up the water spout." Two-year-old Kristin was giving her itsy bitsy spider rendition to a relative on his upper arm. Then he said, "Ouch! The spider bit me!" Kristin turned her head toward his face and asked, "Need an ice pack?" Everyone roared. My tummy is still tickled every time I think of it.

I was driving on a road Jackson didn't recognize. "Grandma Boom, you are on the wrong road."

"No, Jackson, this is a shortcut to where we are going."

"Grandma, sometimes you get lost and take longcuts."

I could not refute what he said. I just laughed.

Ending Salutation to the Grandma Boom Chronicles

I am in my third chapter of a rich life filled with insights, traumas, pain, joy, lessons galore, challenges transformed, and I am aging with a youthening spirit. I am happy. I am grateful. I am also human and would like some things in life to go away or be easier. I want to feel more alive in new ways as I age. I now hearten my perky attitude with my sixty-fifth birthday motto: *More alive at sixty-five*.

I don't know what I don't know, and I get excited about what will come next in my quest to broaden my human potential. My future is determined by the way I live in the present and transform the past. As I age, I want to feel more alive in new ways and I want to help others keep their inner child happy so they can balance out the serious parts of life. When I am no longer living in my body on this planet, I want to leave sparkles in my footsteps.

Blessings of sparkling light to your heart,

Grandma Boom

Have a Slice of Self-Help Pie

Many of us want the world to heal. We want to make it a better place for the generations that come after us. Government budgets could have some impact on the state of the world. But people, individually and collectively, have great power. It comes from using our own internal resources and healing ourselves. *That* is the most powerful way to help heal our planet, our relationships, families, friendships, communities, and countries. It begins with the relationship we have with ourselves.

Self-help is not selfish if it is filled with goodness and does not harm anyone. Love is a creative source that heals. You are lovable. I am lovable. We are all human in our weaknesses and strengths. We are all growing. Love yourself. Self-help is an act of loving yourself, and instilling joy into the process makes it smoother. Enjoy you.

Physical Pain

The initial response to pain is "OUCH!" What happens is that the body tenses up when the mind focuses on the "OUCH" of the pain sensation. This worsens the pain because tension works against the body's response to assist whatever is causing it. Imagine a fire alarm going off. The firemen jump in their truck, and head to put out the fire, but run into a blockade that stops them from getting there. When tension takes hold in the body, it prevents the good circulation of blood flow, stresses the nervous system, tightens muscles, and wreaks havoc on thought processes and emotions. The healing response is delayed, prolonging the pain, sometimes intensifying it. But either way, the mind, body, and emotions work together, whether in response to the OUCH reflex or to the calmer version of pain management.

1. **B•R•E•A•T•H•E**. When you relax and B R E A T H E slowly, deeply, and evenly, it assists the body's system responses, making it easier for them to help the area in pain. A switch is turned on, so to speak, when you breathe through the pain instead of tense against it.

    One technique is to inhale slowly to the count of five, hold for two seconds, and then exhale over the count of five.

    Square breathing is another great technique for focus. Draw a square in your mind as you breathe. Breathe to the count of four going up the left side of the square. Hold to the count of four going across the top side. Exhale to count of four coming down the right side. Then hold to the count of four. Start over. Repeat as necessary.

2. **POSTIVE FOCUS.** It is essential to maintain a positive focus. When you focus on a negative feeling (This hurts terribly, damn it or Why did this happen?) it puts unnecessary stress on the body. If you have pain, slow

down, breathe, and use your mind to help the pain in a positive way. (I am helping my injury. It feels better to relax right now. I have compassion for my foot.) Some people find that focusing on an uplifting image, such as the ocean or a mountain, helps. When I practice pain control during dental surgeries, instead of focusing on the sound of the dental tools, I imagine my grandchildren in a playhouse and making happy sounds.

When a baby cries, we want to soothe it. If we are tense and agitated, the baby will feel this and not calm down. It is the same dynamic with a pained area of the body. It needs soothing.

3. **APPLY PRESSURE ELSEWHERE.** If an area is hurting and you have difficulty taking your mind off the pain, it can help balance your mind's attention if you put a little pressure on another area of your body. Think of it like an acupressure feeling. For example, if your mouth is hurting, use a finger on one hand to apply pressure to your other hand or your leg. Discover what works best for you.

4. **USE YOUR WILL.** Use your volition to program yourself and say, "When I get hurt, I WILL remember to breathe slowly and have compassion for the pain, helping it to heal. Nothing will stop me. I will feel good about myself when I do this. My efforts will bring greater self-confidence and create endorphins." Use your own words.

Use your will to create a healing mechanism inside yourself. It feels great to use mind/body control and develop new skills, regardless of your age.

5. **GRATITUDE.** Last, but not least, feel gratitude. When gratitude is enlivened in the heart center, a flow of energy keeps the heart open. This helps focus the mind in an uplifting way and helps the circulatory system.

Using these techniques will help you to cope with pain and to heal.

Anger

We all have anger. Even the Dalai Lama says he experiences anger. Using it as a tool to release stuck energy is a practice I have found helpful. Anger brings a "note to self" that something unfair or not right according to our thinking has happened and that we would like to control or change it.

- **Locate your anger inside your body.** It starts in one place. When you don't catch it there and do something with it, the anger spreads to other places in the body, eventually encompassing us. When it takes over your body, you lose control. When you become aware of where your anger starts and have decided to release it in a healthy way, you are in control.

- **Use your volition.** Decide now if you want to progress and use anger as a tool to increase self-management and control the damage.

- **Know that your thoughts** are one of your body's signals. If you lose control of them, it may lead to regret and unnecessary stress. When your thoughts become repetitive and you can't stop thinking the angry thoughts, that tells you who is in control. Processing the anger is one thing. Digging in where it hurts is another.

- **Experiment with healthful ways to release anger.** Be creative and vary the options to work with your life circumstances. For example, if you live near others, you may not want to scream as a release unless you do it into a towel or pillow. Please note, there is a difference between screaming as a release and screaming at someone. I am referring to release screaming. Do you need to pound on something? Try pounding a pillow or hammering nails into a log.

- **Jumping up and down** is a great anger release that uses the whole body.

- **Artwork:** Take crayons and scribble the feeling onto the paper with the colors that represent what is going on inside and needs to come out. Or draw/color images that represent the feeling. Looking at your artwork can trigger ways to communicate about your feelings.

- **Communication** is a great mode for anger release if it is done appropriately. Some individuals can release through good communication skills. Others need to release physically first before being able to communicate. Some need silent time alone.

Any of these methods, alone or in combination, will get you started. Not harming anyone or anything is the trick to releasing anger in a healthful way.

- **Know your intention with anger.** Understand your own patterns. How often do you express anger inappropriately by releasing it on innocent parties? How often do you repress it? How often do you use anger in a healthy manner, communicating, releasing, and not causing harm to yourself or others? Know yourself. Be aware. Then you can use anger as a positive tool.

One of the ways I enjoyed releasing anger when I lived in the forest was thorough. I focused on the trigger point that carried the anger in the body. It was my stomach. I imagined there was a fishing line attached to it. In my hand was a thick stick that connected to the fishing line that went into my stomach. I stooped down, focused on the cause of the anger, where I felt it, then jumped up with all my might, screaming the anger out while throwing the stick. I visualized the scream and stick pulling out the anger from my stomach. I could see and feel the power of the anger that had been inside me. This was always a great anger release. Afterward, I was clearer and calmer and could use my communication skills.

Hurt

When we hurt, it envelops the mind, body, and emotions in a significant way. There can be feelings of having been abused, injured, betrayed, violated, damaged, disrespected, not valued. Being hurt is seen as a blow from the outside. Protecting ourselves from undue hurt is wise. But at times, hurt arises without warning. And there are times we do the harm to ourselves with our negative thoughts, feelings, and actions.

1. **Have a plan.** Accept the fact that hurt has happened. Wishing it had not happened is a trap. If you think that thought, release it. Deal with the hurt. Process what is necessary in order to come to some kind of understanding inside yourself and, if possible, with the party that caused the harm. Often times it is not possible to come to an understanding. Betrayal and violation can create the deepest kind of hurt and it can take great effort to heal.

2. **Step back.** See clearly. Seeing that anyone who hurts, betrays, or harms in any way is not happy or healthy brings some objectivity.

3. **Forgiveness** is key to fully releasing the harm. It does not mean that engaging with the person you forgive is necessary. It can heal in a relationship, but ultimately you are the one who carries the tension of a grudge or the freedom of forgiveness. Forgiveness heals you. It happens in your heart.

4. **One important key is to notice what you do with the hurt caused by someone else**. Do you prolong it? Do you fuel it? Is it a factor that will debilitate your self-worth or confidence? Know your patterns and your truth. Know what you want to do with the hurt. Dedicate it to a good cause, such as healing self-sabotage or the tendency to feel sorry for yourself. Allowing the hurt to stay too long means it will camp inside you and cramp other aspects of life. How long is too long? You decide. Take action. You can heal your hurt if you choose to. It takes time. Get help if needed. Listen to your body signs and your thoughts. Learn a lesson and polish some skills in dealing with

the hurt. Two roads are available to you: downtrodden spirit or healing and self-love. If you choose healing, take steps. It is always and only up to you.

5. **Move the energy.** Be creative. Develop options. You can draw or color the hurt. Locate it in your body. Imagine a healing salve doctoring it, healing it. Color that. Write down the components of the healing salve. For example: self-kindness, humor, the essence of beauty. Stretch your imagination. Steeping in the hurt too long will make it more difficult to heal. It is still possible to heal. It is always and only up to you.

6. **Be aware of thoughts, feelings, and intentions** that cause self-harm. Forgive yourself. Take action. Heal yourself. It is empowering for your well-being and will help to uplift you. No need to be hard on yourself. It takes time. You are worth it.

Depression

In 2010, over 200 million prescriptions were written for depression in the United States for adults, teens, and children. Think about it. What do we need to change? Where are we going as a society, as a family, as individuals?

1. **Know the signs.** Depressed energy pulls a person downward, giving her/him sloping shoulders and droopy, downcast eyes. The person maintains a sluggish attitude that often borders on hopelessness or a total lack of motivation. Creative energy does the opposite. It creates an upsurge through the body that expands

the mind and the chest, opens the eyes, and increases energy levels. The heart is bright and open.

2. **Know the cause of depression.** It may be something you have no control over. Decide if you would like to move out of that depressed state. Once you decide, there are many options. Some people do require medical assistance and medication. Many do not need it. Find ways that speak to you to move the stuck energy of depression. Everyone must find her/his own formula. If you are depressed and what you are doing isn't working, it is not as easy to keep trying. If possible, find someone who can assist you either professionally or as a friend.

3. **Some techniques.** One of the techniques I have thoroughly enjoyed is to take one hand, and tap on the crown of the head while at the same time, tapping on the sternum. Do this for 3-5 minutes. If your hands tire, switch them. The sternum point opens up all the energy meridians in the body for better energy flow. The top of the head sends signals all the way down the spine and through energy centers, which are called chakras. You begin to move energy all through the body. Notice how you feel after doing this. It can be done as much as needed. It is natural, takes time, and helps you to help yourself.

Another exercise is to slowly stretch your hands and arms up and out to make a large V with them. Look up toward the sky. BREATHE in slowly and exhale slowly as you say something that feels good to you and similar to, "I am open to feeling uplifted." Do this with as many breaths as possible, holding the V position. When your arms tire, let them rest. Repeat exercise as much as needed. You can do this exercise and follow with the head and sternum tapping. It is all about moving energy and redirecting it.

Of course, seek outside help when needed. Talk to someone. Exercise and eat well. Use your will. Fresh air is important, too. When medication is required, also do other things to support your system as it comes out of depression. Relying solely on medication only temporarily helps with symptoms and not the root cause.

Dealing with Circumstances Beyond Your Control

There is something to be said for the eye of the storm. Swirling energies in circumstances that seem wildly out of control, or even mildly out of control, can grab us and give us psychic whiplash. When you feel like you are being yanked from one place to another, it is easy to feel victimized. At that point, we weaken and feel that we have no control.

While you may not have any power to control the circumstances around you, it is essential to realize you always have a choice about how you handle your inner world. Being centered and grounded, focusing your thoughts, and feeling a calm center inside of you while maintaining slow, deep, even breathing, and stretching can make a world of difference.

- Decide you want to find a way to feel stable in the swirling of circumstances that are out of control. Until you make that decision, you will not find your way. Helping yourself starts inside your mind with a feeling of determination. Notice where that decision is felt in your body. It is a place of strength you can go back to and rely upon.

- See yourself grounded in the earth with deep roots far down into the earth's core. Breathe that in. Feel it. See yourself and feel yourself aligned like a strong tree. While the wind of circumstances may blow your branches, your core is steady. Feel it.

- If it is possible to step out of the situation, take a break to clear your head. Massage, acupuncture, acupressure, reflexology, going for a hike ... whatever helps you. Give yourself help to support your self-help.

- Ask for help when you need it.

- Offer your situation up in dedication to something or someone that touches your heart. That helps keep you motivated.

Intuition

You have it. We all do. It is a matter of acknowledging it.

- Listen to the inner voice of intuition, your instinctual knowledge and natural sense.

- If you act on intuition, you will feel better than if you ignore it, which leads to regret.

- Each person has her/his own way of knowing and feeling intuition. Think of it as natural instinct. I get a feeling in my heart, sometimes also in my stomach. It is important to learn how to discriminate between your emotions and your intuition.

- Practice will help you to learn to discriminate. Intuition has more of a fleeting sense to it that can become repetitive. For example, not feeling right about going on a trip but not knowing why. Listening to that inner voice, you may discover why, or you may not, but you will feel relieved. If it is an emotional decision about not wanting to go on a trip, you will know the reason. Desire is not intuition. Hate is not intuition. Resentment is not intuition. Neither are longing, jealousy, fear, or many other emotions. Listen to your own inner voice and to the way your thoughts-feelings-intentions work. Realize you can control your emotions if they don't control you. Trust yourself. And polish your intuition. Intuition is not a control-based experience. It happens as a receptivity to more than what your five physical senses register.

- Practice paying attention and you will become more skilled. You can ask your inner voice or guidance to help you develop your intuitive abilities. Intention makes a difference in the skill level. Paying attention also makes a difference.

Teaching Children About Self-Help

Deep breathing
Research has proven that with short, irregular breaths we take in one to two pints of oxygen as fuel for the mind and body. Slow, deep abdominal breathing brings in six to seven pints of oxygen. Getting insufficient oxygen means being tense, negative, having greater difficulty making decisions, not thinking clearly … the list goes on. Getting sufficient oxygen means that it is easier to be positive, think clearly, have fun, and make good decisions.

You can use bubbles
Slow, deep, even breathing means you have more calm control with your breath. That will make *big* bubbles. Short, irregular, tense breaths will make small bubbles. Children can see and feel the difference. Teach them how to breathe in through their belly buttons, filling the abdomen (not the chest) to the count of five. Hold for two counts. Then exhale slowly to the count of five. Do this several times. Talk about the difference in how you all feel when you are tense and when you are calm.

Knot and sock
Get a jute or rough rope and make a knot for the child to hold in one hand. Get a soft sock to hold in the other hand. Have the child make a tense face, feeling hard and tight like

the knot. Then have her/him take a deep breath and relax and untie the knots in her/his face, exhaling slowly to feel soft like the sock. Repeat with different body parts so that the child can see and feel the difference for her-/himself.

Tense/Relax or calm game

A fun way to teach young children about the difference between the feeling/concept of tension and its opposite, a calm/relaxed feeling, is to have a fun experience they won't forget. With young children, get on the floor on all fours. Choose an animal, such as a dog. Direct the children to get tense and upset like a dog would be, making tense dog faces and sounds. Bark and growl together. Next, have them take slow, deep, even breaths with you, filling up their belly buttons with oxygen and counting to five. Hold this breath for two counts. Exhale while counting to five. Now become relaxed, calm dogs. Point out how different it feels, looks, and sounds to be calm instead of tense. Choose another animal to do the same with—monkeys, cats, cows. Children love coming up with animals. Point out when you are tense like an upset dog in everyday life and need to take a deep breath. This reinforces the lesson, experience, and image.

Inner-Body awareness

Use examples in everyday life to help the child become more conscious of inner body awareness. "I felt a tight knot in my shoulders when I couldn't find my keys. I took a deep breath so I wouldn't stay upset and I felt calm again while I looked for my keys." Helping children to have inner awareness gives them more choices inside themselves, regardless of external circumstances. Using yourself as a role model gives them reinforcement, encouragement, and the idea that this is a good way to live. More awareness equals having more choices.

Breathing march

Use a jingle to march around with children. Whole body learning makes a huge difference in the absorption and retention of a lesson. You can march and sing outdoors, indoors, with drums or without, ringing bells to the jingle, or being creative in other ways. Teach children that when we have calm self-control with deep breathing, we can think better and make good choices.

March to: BREATHE, THINK AND MAKE A GOOD CHOICE. Repeat this multiple times while marching with or without instruments. It is the whole body learning experience that aids in absorption and retention.

I highly recommend my *Superkid Power Guidebook* (www. grandmaboom.com), which is filled with techniques to teach children to tap their own Superkid Power and use their inner resources. Many themes are addressed, including anger, stress, sadness, and jealousy. Other books that reinforce skills in story-form that I developed over forty years, getting feedback from children, parents, and teachers, are also available. Enjoy!

"You are where you are
because of who you are.

You are who you are because
of what you think."

~ ERNEST HOLMES

Firm up Life's Muscles with Affirmations

In a nutshell, affirmations help retrain your mind in a positive way. But there are several things you need to remember and focus on in order for these to serve you well. Use a positive focus in the present tense, as if your intention has already been accomplished.

"I AM" are the best words to use at the beginning of the affirmation. The word "NOW" is best used at the end of the affirmation. "I AM _____[healed, happy, grateful, prosperous, successful, etc.] NOW." When initially establishing the affirmation, you should repeat it as many as 100 times, or more as needed. Use it frequently. For example, if you are focusing on something long term, create time every day and for an extended period, for example, two months, to use the affirmation(s). If you are focusing on something short term, determine how much you can dedicate to the affirmation(s) each day for a week or two. It is up to you to get a sense of how much is needed. There is no limit.

Most important, *feel* the affirmation. It is the emotional body that registers the most powerful and passionate energy, which in turn helps to set the affirmation in motion for its eventual manifestation.

Set aside your complaints. If your attitude or thoughts are riddled with complaints about what you do not have yet—for example, healing, prosperity—it works against the forward motion of affirmation.

More examples of affirmations:

I AM PEACEFUL NOW.

I AM FILLED WITH HUMBLE GRATITUDE NOW.

I AM OPEN TO HIGHER GUIDANCE NOW.

I AM A CREATIVE PERSON NOW.

I AM FULFILLED NOW.

I AM STRONG NOW.

I AM H EALED NOW.

I AM RECEPTIVE TO THE RIGHT PATH NOW.

I AM FILLED WITH LIGHT NOW

I AM LOVE NOW.

I AM LOVING NOW.

I AM TAKING THE STEPS FOR SUCCESS NOW.

I AM KINDNESS NOW.

I AM OWNING MY POWER AND FEEL FULLY ALIVE NOW.

I AM STRENGTHENING WHO I AM NOW.

I AM EXERCISING MY INNER CHILD TO BE MORE ALIVE NOW.

I AM YOUTHENING MY SPIRIT NOW.

I AM FORGIVING THOSE WHO CAUSED HARM NOW.

I AM GRATEFUL FOR ALL I AM LEARNING NOW.

I AM ABUNDANCE IN ALL ASPECTS OF MY LIFE NOW.

I AM FEARLESS NOW.

I AM COURAGE NOW.

Acknowledgements

Adventuring into the creation of this book meant a small village would evolve to support its birthing. I am especially grateful to expert literary midwives, Chris Molé for her guiding visionary design gifts, Patricia Florin for her egoless editorial expertise, and Larissa Kyzer for her sharpness in proofreading.

Danny Lockwood, I heart you and your soul touching mastery. Charley Cullen Walters, you amazed me with your endearing assistance. Trent Vanegas, thank you for connecting with the spirit of who I am. My family, especially, my grandchildren, children, son-in-law, sister and her family—we are fortunate to be family. Thank you for all that it has required in our work and play and learning together through the years. To my ancestors, I wish I were wiser when you were here to more fully appreciate your gifts. Deep appreciation goes to those who share true friendship. It pours life nectar into our vessels, making us heart-wealthy beyond measure.

A special thanks to all my mentors for having faith in me and helping me to persevere. My deep gratitude to the children and their parents who have trusted me to help them in their struggles. Emmet Fox's materials have nourished me with miracles.

Humbly, I thank the Source of Life and all unseen assistance throughout my life journey.

Mother Nature, you're the best

© SUZANNE WOOD
PHOTOGRAPY

Finally! I appreciate myself for being willing to be happy and to adventure into my potential.

About the Author

Vibrant and excited to be 65, Janai Mestrovich's passion for human potential and stress-prevention has been a 40-year journey. With a Master's Degree in Family and Child Development, she is a pioneer in children's stress-prevention programs, an author, newspaper columnist, TV producer / host/creator/writer, and international speaker. Janai's awards and honors include: Silver Medal, NY International Film and Television Festival; Most Innovative Children's Program, Oregon; Miss Hospitality of Kansas, 1969; watermelon seed spitting champion. Her quest in human potential includes pain control and intuitive development. She is an advocate for furthering holistic education for children, and delights in being an outrageously fun grandmother.

Janai has taught at the University of Oregon, global conferences, and daycare settings, where she encourages all, young and old alike, to engage their joy-filled inner child, and tap into the freedom of holistic aging.

"Dance when you're broken.
Dance, if you've torn the bandage off.
Dance in the middle of the fighting.
Dance in your blood.
Dance when you're perfectly free."

~ RUMI

Photo Gallery

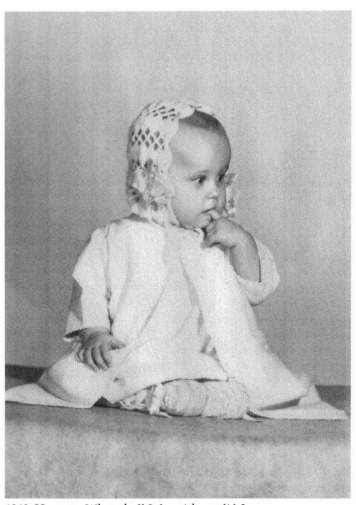

1949, Hmmm. What shall I do with my life?

Mom and Dad married June 21, 1947, hoping for a good life.

50th Anniversary. They made it through storms, good times, separation, differences and determination.

The beginning of love for ocean play.

Mom is fixing salmon patties, grits and okra for supper.

I'm sleeping on marbles tonight to get dimples since I'm flat chested, called "Uglystick" and got a hole in my head.

Mom's mouth from the south could not be ignored. "You better give your soul to God because your ass is mine."

Mom, Procter & Gamble main receptionist and switchboard operator. If someone was nasty, she unplugged them!

Big Mama, Ida Harrison, Mom's Mom.

Major John Jan Mestrovich, WWII. "I learned there was a time to kill or be killed."

Ted and me. We were Wild Bill Hickock and
Annie Oakley until he shot me.

Childhood home, Miros Circle, with basement for tornado
protection.

Ted, Karen, Dad, Mom, Johnny, Jannie (Janai)

Mama (paternal Croatian grandmother) and me being cozy.

Uncle Mark, Papa, Baby Dad, Mama, Aunt Kay

Handsome Dad, Mama, Papa. Back row: Uncle Mark, Aunt Kay

My younger sister was always special to me.

1966. Wild Canadian portage. I am dipping a leaf into the lake and drinking

I wrote to the Kennedy's at the White House requesting a
photo. They signed it personally.

Unanimously voted Miss Hospitality of Kansas, 1969, by contestants. Televised.

Yes, circa 1990, I was a pimple for Halloween.

In heaven, pregnant with first child, daughter,
in comfy footy pajamas.

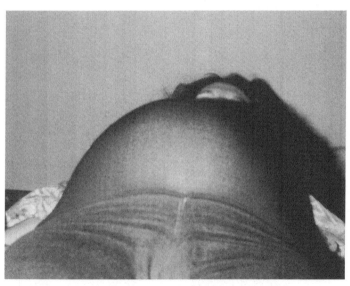

Pregnant with second child, son. Couldn't see my feet.

Darion turns one. Celebrated by his sister, cousin, Aliah, and me.

Darion, 2, learning to roll out dough for Croatian povetica.

WHAT I LOOK AND FEEL LIKE INSIDE MYSELF WHEN I DON'T
CHOOSE TO RELAX MY EXTRA TENSION

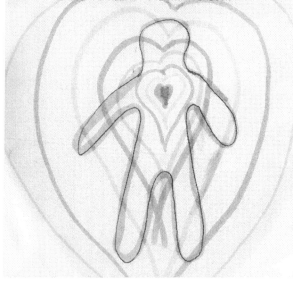

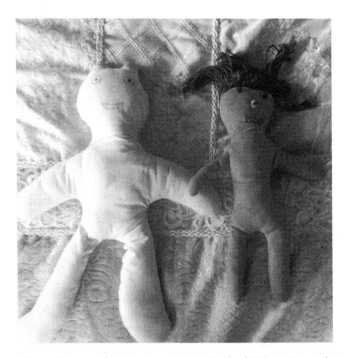

Above: Homeschooling project for both children: Draw/
design, cut out, stuff, sew dolls

Left: Home school inner body awareness artwork.
Children color what tension/stress looks like inside
their bodies and what it looks and feels like to be calm
to show contrast. This is used in all my work with
children.

1984. Teaching preschoolers self-calming techniques. Son, Darion, niece, Aliah on either side of me. Sheila Embers in circle.

Mid 1990's Self-Help Program, Drain, Oregon, K-3. Cassie Ruud and Shelby N. with me.

Training Health Division at American Embassy, Lima, Peru

2013: Teaching preschoolers self-management skills about lying.

Lie Ball: What it looks and feels like. 3D learning for kids so they know how they harm themselves when they lie and where they feel it inside the body.

2014: Teaching preschoolers Self-Help stress management skills as a fun fairy, of course!

Singing it out at my daughter's wedding: Me, Karen, Mom

Pure joy becoming Grandma Boom.

2014: Repeat dress-ups 30 years later. Me, son, daughter.

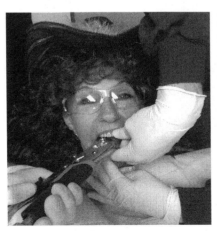

Pain control. Implant stuck. Dentistry tools failed. No meds. No joke.

Transformed SAD to GLAD. Fun at airport saying goodbye to son, Darion, at Xmas.

I live with Bozo. He lets me bop him to get my anger out.

Sunglass right eye popped out suddenly onto a stranger.
Lucille Ball is my patron saint.

2014: Refusing to be
boring living alone.
Selfie snowball fight.

2013: Celebrating 62 years of annual wave riding in Ixtapa.
Sand burn on my knees. Worth the burn!

Seed spitting with friend, Maya. I won but she's pretty good.

Dress-ups: Doorway to ageless play and freedom.
Chronological years, 65. Inner child years: any age I want.

Found new ways to hang on during major life transitions. And laugh! If Mom was still around she'd laugh and then tell me to act like a lady! Haha

Xmas Fairy in lights, Ashland Festival of Lights parade, 2013. Battery packs on top of my head and in other discreet locations. Welcomed son home at airport dressed like this!

2013: Attending Loy and Ryan's wedding, I granted wishes as the wedding fairy. With Will Sawyer and Jim Key.

60th Birthday as Cleopatra. Dress-ups with Darion, and *BELLO Magazine* publishers, Alek Tomovic and Steph Marquet.

64th birthday. Cloris Leechman teaches me to take my first "shot" EVER. Darion, flabbergasted. B-52 in a double shot glass.

64th birthday. Lily Tomlin, very sweet soul, doing photos.

Charley Cullen Walters and Sebastian Z. Leal don dress-ups at my 65th birthday party.

Special 65th birthday dinner with Trent Vanegas (www.pinkisthenewblog.com), birthday girl, Darion Lowenstein

Loy Rackley, Omar Bousquet, Darion Lowenstein and SuperMom at Darion's surprise superhero party.

2014: Jumping out of box as SuperMom to surprise Darion for surprise superhero birthday party hosted at Fred & Jason's.

Sheila and Kristin doing dress-ups at my 65th.

More fun winging it at my 65th Birthday party with: Rob Tisinai, Will Nixon, Rodrigo Torrres, Me, Scotland Beavers, Roger Henry, Matthew Passmore.

After sister, Karen's two kids' weddings this spring, we needed silly play time!

Dancing as the Autumn Fairy!
Photo by Pam Danielle Photography, Ashland, Oregon

2014: Freedom Fairy, July 4th parade, 2nd place winner in adult entries, Ashland, OR. Bringing joy to the crowd.

2013: Ashland Monster one mile Marathon. 2nd place costume winner.

Eclectic Medicine Wheel I made for sacred healing space in forest.

Janai Mestrovich's Children's Materials can be found at www.grandmaboom.com

Superkid Power Guidebook: Parents! Teachers! Help Empower Kids to: *develop self-care and emotional intelligence *self-control making good choices *build self-confidence with stress management skills *build inner strengths and self-responsibility Only moments per week!

Dragonella: *Ages 4-8.* Magical and entertaining! Claire's special friends only she can see, the Sky Dragons, help her to magically transform into Dragonella. They fly to distant lands where Claire discovers how to help others solve problems. Wonderful stories with great messages! Beautiful illustrations!

Beeing Calm: Coloring story book. Delightful story teaching self-calming skills with a bumble bee.

Superkid Saves the Day. Interactive: *Ages 4-8.* Magical and entertaining! Stories with skills AND accompanying questions to ask as you go. Included are "hands-on" activities for the child to do. A great way to open up a dialogue about important feelings in a safe fun way!

Superkid Camp: *Interactive. Ages 4-8.* At Superkid Camp kids from different cultures learn that all kids have problems and can make good choices using self-help skills. Kids learn to respect others who may look or live differently than themselves, regardless of skin color, religion, style of home or clothing. Entertaining stories demonstrate skills with sharing, communicating feelings, ridicule, blame, and more.

Jackson's Fun Adventures. I Can Be What I Want To Be: *Preschool - K.* The magic box with costumes in Jackson's Fun Adventures delights children. A boy finds himself inside a new costume every day which leads him through many ways of exploring what it is like to be in different roles. He discovers through his imagination that he can be whatever he wants to be.

Check out Grandma Boom's children's materials and youtube videos at **grandmaboom.com**

30170672R00173

Made in the USA
San Bernardino, CA
22 March 2019